In God's Name

I0415215

The Great Game

Another Religious Crusade, Conquest
Over The Dead With All Rights To Rape
and Plunder,,, still going on today.

Control – Oil - Power

Socialosity

Socialosity

Social Nervosa Delusion

Socialosity

Socialosity

The Madness Found Within All Societies
And the parallels between

A Sequel to the book
Scrupulosity

Written & Illustrated b
William J. Ryan

Socialosity

Socialosity is an affliction that we all suffer from, including you, the reader. Yes, the one that is *looking for the one and only flaw within these pages so as to discount the entire concept*, point or conclusions drawn. You cannot absorb any information with pre-disposed conclusions or if you speed read. Skipping over the parts that you think you already know,,, but don't because, all your life, you have skipped over the words *subconsciously looking past anything that will shatter your world*. Thereby with those lifelong actions, you have created a sealed container of which you have become comfortable in, safe and secure with the perceived (delusion) of those fellow sufferers. Its time to step out of your homemade container and enter new unfamiliar lands that are dangerous and most times vary scary. *I can only hope the truth will set you free as it has me.*

Introduction

What is the driving force in our lives that forces us to do things we know are wrong, then after we do them we must live with those actions (our actions) for the rest of our lives? The images forever live in the shadows and recesses of our minds,,, hiding them from the eyes of the rest of the world, pretending to be normal.

The weak ones can justify and pray to one god or another for strength and forgiveness. But the other lost souls know the truth; they can't hide behind the thin vial of religion. They end up taking their own lives in order to free themselves from the ghosts of their actions that have haunted them.

The doors in our minds that cover over the black oozing holes in our souls, the damage we have done to ourselves (based upon our concept of reality), constantly creak open. We spend a lifetime trying to keep them closed, hidden from others prying judgmental eyes.

Within the pages of this book, I try to examine the many causes of these oozing sores within our souls; *which were many times self-inflicted*. They are actually caused by the **Deceivers** *(sociopath, psychopath)* that are all around us *who always seem to rise to the top*. We can't and won't see what is going on, because we are caught up in all the distractions that were deliberately set in place to cause us to stumble. We struggle with these unanswered questions based upon half-truths and twisted lies, all of our lives.

There is a method to the madness orchestrated by the sociopathic/psychopathic rich and powerful that control us. When exposed to the light of truth, their power over us is taken away. But you must first think,,, no,,, know that there is a problem.

The problem is,,, all of our lives we have been lied to from our earliest memories to this day, by the Deceivers. Some of these creatures have risen up into religions like the – Jesuit. A satanic group founded in 1540 that took over the Roman Catholic Church in 1586 and left their mark with the Egyptian Obelisk set in St. Peter's Square.

Why is that important? The Obelisk is a secretive religion based on the Sun God Satan and this obelisk worships Lucifer.

From the Jesuit Oath:

"To be a spy even among your own brethren; to believe no man, to trust no man.

"Obtaining their confidence, to seek even to preach from their pulpits, and to denounce withal the vehemence in you nature our holy religion and the Pope; and even to descend so low as to become a Jew among Jews.

"as I am directed to do, to extirpate and exterminate them from the face of the whole earth; and that I will spare neither age, sex or condition; and that I will hang, waste, boil, flay, strangle and bury alive these infamous heretics, rip up the stomachs and wombs of their woman and crush their infants heads against the walls,"

Is this a loving god or Satan?

Chapters

Socialosity

Chapter One

Introduction to Scrupulosity

"God help me"

What is it that makes us do things that we know are insane?

Why is it ok to push away others?

Socialosity

It should be known at the beginning of this book that I am an autodidact layman (self-taught), trying to understand the **accepted insanity** of people all around the world. I start with what I know. The gullibility of people and religion truly baffles me to no end. I don't get people.

As I have said many times, I always end up going in a different direction from my intended direction. I call it my **A B C** theory. I start out at point **A**, and look towards point **B** (as a goal), and then I begin to head for it. On the way, I see point **C** and end up going there, never stopping at point **B**, passing it by. I never would have seen point **C** had I not headed for point **B**. One must move forward if one is to ever learn,,, you cannot stand still.

Case example is my book Scrupulosity; wherein I personally wanted to understand the madness that we all can see in all religions, but look the other way, ignoring its horrific actions in the name of one god or another. A perfect example is the Christian religion and their 8th commandment of god, "*Thou shalt not kill.*" Yet, Christians across the globe are killing Muslims in the name of one god or another. To me, looking from the outside of religion, I see the Muslims only defending themselves, their land and their culture from the invading Christians around the world. Seems to be another 200 plus year Christian crusade; killing and stealing the wealth of another country,,, so they can control its people and money, pushing its religion upon them.

Today I know another more sinister power has created the FAKE grounds for war from 9/11 as the people behind it think 'let my enemies kill my enemies' (Christian vs. Islam),,, and we are.

To say nothing, not point this out to others would be an act of insanity for me. I have spent a lifetime trying to understand and find the truth among all the lies from the many **Deceivers**. All of us on this planet are swimming in and drowning in lies and half-truths. For me, I just had to start in one place and that place was religion. *It's the greatest power over most all of us.*

Point of clarification; my religion is NONE OF THE ABOVE. I am not a Christian, a Jew, a Muslim, an agnostic or an atheist. I am none of the above and that permits me to move freely from one religion to another without prejudice and with an open and sometimes critical mind.

Quite by accident, I discovered the word **Scrupulosity,** the only information I could find just did not seem to fit the present day meaning. We can see by the insane actions of the religious, their man made disorder.

The term is derived from the Latin word **scrupulum**, *a sharp stone, implying a stabbing pain on the conscience mind*.

What a great word!

This 6500 year old word helps explain so much. Just think of all the insane actions of religious people around the world, then look to home,,, in your own back yard. You may find yourself wallowing in your own black oozing pit of religious lies and half-truths, meant to control you, your actions, your children and your money.

But you have to look.

At this point you are probably having a difficult time keeping your religion at bay, pushing back the ancient words of the sheep and goat herder that wrote the words you live by. Put them down,,, you must to see the truth.

A religion may have started out good, but the sociopaths, the psychopaths and the pedophiles have taken over most every religion and government in the world.

Look and you will see just how Satanism would appear to have taken over Judaism, Christianity and as of 2007, Islam. Look for the Obelisk around the world and you will find the Sun God Satan and its all seeing eye of Lucifer.

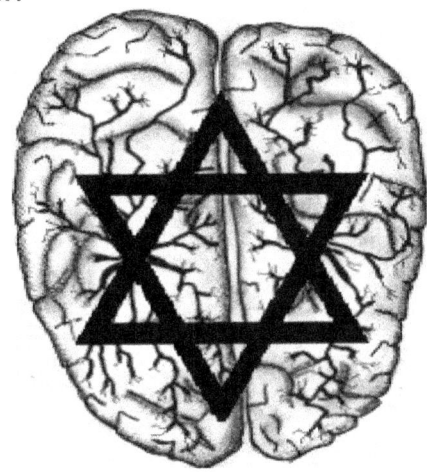

Scrupulosity: a sharp cutting stone within the mind.

What did the creators of this word see that made them create the word?

Latium is a small region on the coast of west central Italy and dates back to around the 6th century BC, (Christian time). Its language is still used to this very day within the legal community and some religions. Now you have to go back in time and think about the religious people that would have been walking around at that time.

Before the wide acceptance (or *crippling* need) of an old man in the sky, people must have lived an idyllic life. No one was trying to force god upon the children, brainwashing them for life. No one was willingly killing their neighbor because of their religion (or lack of,,, or the wrong one) and justifying their actions of looting and plundering in the name of some god. *What a wonderful time it must have been on Earth,,, without god and this man made disorder.*

However, at this time there were some strange people walking around that believed that they were superior, (*truly believing each man on earth of their religion is a god themselves*) sticking to themselves, believing all the others,,, the **Goyim** (all of us that are not Jewish),,, had defective souls; the **Goy.** Each were less than the cattle in the fields,,, put on earth to serve them,,, the Jewish god people. Keeping to themselves, praying to this old man in the sky. These Jewish people could be seen walking the streets chanting out loud to themselves. Sometimes praying,,, and talking to walls. **Most bizarre!!!**

If you have ever watched a Jew pray or worse yet,,, a room full of Jews praying to their god, it looked to me, the true meaning of the term,,, **Snake Pit**,,, from that of a mental institution. In these times, even to this day,,, when you watch people reciting these words over and over to themselves,,, their actions are truly most bazaar *on a real creepy level.*

Their fear of something as common as death has forced them to endure a lifetime of fear and insane chanting rituals. All of that to insure them a place in a land called heaven,,, away from the **Goyim** and their defective souls.

Point of calefaction: In Jew heaven each Jewish man is entitled to 800 to 2800 slaves. What kind of heaven does that sound like to you? A land of love or a land of hell meant to enslave? None the less, is this a place you want to go to after your life is over,,, into servitude?

These religious people would have been the **Walking Dead** of that time. Cursed to a life of superiority and authority by their religion (their god), to do anything they wanted to the Goy,,, for their god gave them the Goyim to do as they wish, including kill them without retribution. They did and still are to this day committing genocide in Palestine while most of the world looks the other way.

My goal when I researched and wrote **Scrupulosity** was to have an understanding of this word at a more in-depth level. To me, it is clear there is a pattern that forms boxes that can be overlaid upon each religion and the common patterns found within each shows the insanity therein. When overlaid with the common patterns of other religions, they (these boxes or patterns) point out the insanity found within all religions.

Scrupulosity level One

The acceptance of illogical nonsense (gibberish), such as speaking in tongues, god coming to earth to have a baby, the seas parting, or turning water into wine as real is gullibility,,, insanity in itself. All religions to some are just a cult designed to control people and get their money, and I would like to add, endorsed by governments and monarchies alike in order to control the masses. *A good example is all of the Christian crusades that were nothing more than land grabs to enrich the church and kill off the opposition.* The true damage, the true crime is when this insane idiocy is pushed upon children when they are born and later in Sunday BRAIN-washing School.

Scrupulosity level Two:

The individual that has accepted the ignorance of this cult, now seeks out others with the same affliction,,, the same belief, same fears, the same weakening man made mental disorder,,, this OCD (obsessive compulsive disorder) or what I call **Mental Addictive Cancer**,,, <u>need to belong</u>. They began to openly pray in public,,, like the Jews did in Latina (*birth place of the language Latin*). Pushing their madness upon others, and anyone challenging their **mass hysteria** would face their anger, their revenge, as they,,, as a mob,,, defend their ludicrous, bazaar and insane religious actions. *All with* *the god given right to take, rape and kill,,, in the name of their god. Whatever that god is,,, including present day Satan that is controlling most all religions and governments.*

Scrupulosity level Three:

At this level, this man-made mental addictive, cancerous disorder, has now grown into such a sickness of the mind (sharp cutting stone) that people dedicate their lives to the madness of,,, *fear of living and fear of dying*, that it totally consumes their lives. Their leaders now wear garments that distinguish them from the flock, vowing a life of poverty, yet surrounded in riches, living the life of Kings. They stand next to god,,, delivering god's words *(or pretending to, as the Jesuits do),* as they interpret the words in their own way. Self-enrichment, superiority and castles in the sky are their rewards,,, *and let us not forget all the slaves*. One does not even have to believe in god,,, they just need to pretend,,, go through the motions, to enrich themselves.

"You have been taught to insidiously plant the seeds of jealousy and hatred between communities, provinces and states that were at peace, and incited them to deeds of blood, (9/11, 2001) involving them in war with each other, and to create revolutions (Arab Spring 2010) and civil wars in countries that were independent and prosperous."

Jesuit Oath

Scrupulosity Level Four:

This is clearly the most dangerous and deadly level of all. Deep within the dark back rooms, away from the eyes of the flock are the deals meant to enrich the religion and kill off any other religion that in their demented **(sociopath, psychopath, pedophile)** minds,,, threatens them and their wealth. All opposing religions, even if it is similar (same gods) must be destroyed and their property acquired (stolen). A good example is when a child raping priest *(an act of their Right of Passage)* can live freely within a religion without retribution. Thus attracting pedophiles to the cult, because their actions of sexual aggression,,, rape of a child, go unpunished. They are protected within the cult if they push god on the rest of the flock, requiring only to be concealed so as to cultivate new child victims.

God helps those that
help themselves

Jesuits,,, Militia of the POPE

"Make and wage relentless war"

It was after I had finished this book and the 4 levels of insanity within most all religions, that I started to apply this same thinking to other situations. Then it became clear that there were other examples of this same style of illness, the same madness within other societal clicks or cults.

Each like organization has its followers and requirements to become one of them; you must accept their beliefs,,, to wear the badge,,, the cross,,, the uniform and then to possess the power. For me it was then that I could see parallels in scrupulosity,,, and I needed a new term to describe the same disorder found within **Scrupulosity**,,, and I call it *Socialosity*.

Look closely at the levels just described for Scrupulosity, remove religion and apply them to an institution,,, such as the military or the police force. There are so many similarities that it is most disturbing. What I know about the police and the crimes they commit against the rest of us, makes me fear them. Every day they are committing crimes and covering them up. They shoot unarmed people every day and when they (if ever) are brought up on charges,,, they never go to jail. They have a license to kill and they are killing us,,, freely.

Their cult,,, their religion is filled with platitudes of **protect and serve**. When in reality it should be to **shoot first**,,, ask questions later, then **build a case**,,, and put it in a **frame**. Always protecting each other, (those within the cult) even **lying in a court of law** in order to win a case.

The **injustice** we see every day is dividing the nation, as laws are enforced when it is convenient or for the benefit of the cult. Never for the public, "We, the People," if it is to cost too much money, making the law pointless and bringing about underlining vigilantly street justice.

The federal government is preparing for just such an outbreak of dissidence, as the people arm themselves. They are working on the completion of the **FEMA Death Camps**. Or as they may refer to them as relocation camps,,, relocating us under six feet of dirt.

FEMA Death Camps

Where all Christians are welcomed with open arms.

Remember… "Obey your government!!!"

Socialosity

Chapter Two

Insanity
All around Us

In The Near Future

As of 2017, it is estimated that over two million people, families,,, have moved away from society (corruption, drugs) and all the insanity it brings, to live Off Grid, away from the social insanity and delusions of others.

$\mathbf{F}$or those of us that actually use our intelligence to think and reason,,, we often find ourselves scratching our heads, wondering why things are the way they are. From Global Warming and **lying politicians** all the way to **corruption** within our judicial system, the human species has learned to look the other way or just run. There is so much deception within our global society that it is becoming an art form and these deceptive skills are passed on from generation to generation in what is called, **Business School**. I call it the art of willfully taking advantage of someone else, for personal gain and profit,,, sometimes also called the **Free Market System**.

These atrocities are becoming so common place that we don't even openly acknowledge them anymore. There are so many in recent years that one could specialize in one type and become an expert in that field of crimes against society, for the self-protection of the individual(s) assets,,, example; Opiates.

As a layman, my personal expertise is found within the field of overall tendencies, actions and patterns that lead to open group dysfunction (those boxes I speak of that hold trapped people), crimes and the cover up of same, if found to be somehow wrong when compared to other social patterns or lifestyles. It is so easy to look the other way or just say, *"Its someone's else's problem,"* when in fact, saying nothing,,, doing nothing,,, is another dysfunctional antisocial pattern. Doing nothing rewards this bad behavior and the problem(s) just grows. *That is precisely what the sociopaths, the psychopaths and pedophiles want you to do,,, look the other way,,, or better yet,,, join them!!!*

Due to the sheer magnitude of crimes against society,,, those of us that don't commit crimes, think it is truly understandable to just walk away. But I have found there is a common global underlying mental disorder. I wonder, are we born with this or are we to learn it as children within the games we are taught to play? Lessons learned and passed on without consciously knowing or possibly brought with us within our spirit at birth; most likely from previous lives, but that is a question asked by others.

How **Socialosity** occurs is almost a moot point, for it is all around us if we will just open our eyes and look. I would add, the need for social activity is within every spirit,,, **like** creatures flock together, (birds of a feather).

The insanity,,, the level of dysfunction of a society will determine its ability to survive. If injustice is permitted to occur and not rectified, faith in that system begins to fail and that society will began to erode away. We pull back, looking for a better system, free of the **Deceivers** (sociopaths, psychopaths) that have a vested interest,,, profit,,, in the current system. That is occurring today, *"If the government can cheat me,,, I can cheat the government."* Therein lies the problem,,, for if BIG corporations can cheat the government out of taxes,,, so can the little guy.

The Internal Revenue Service is a foreign stock company and every cent paid to the United States

Treasury goes overseas. Not a cent is ever spent on this country. The Supreme Court has ruled no less than 4 times that the IRS is an illegal tax and unconstitutional. 4 times!

These **Deceivers**,,, the best,,, move freely from one society to another, for that is the nature of **Socialosity** and it is an international dysfunction. After entering one society,,, like a virus or parasite,,, and finding the society's flaws, one looks for another to spread their venom through and take over the host,,, thereby killing it,,, *"make and wage relentless war."* **Parasitical Societies** are all around us, but we have to look to see them.

One such example of parasitical societies is most **all** religions. As we hope for an idyllic life, our dreams are dashed as we find they too are corrupted with **Deceivers** from top to bottom. The choice is to stay and look the other way or move on, spending a lifetime in the search for an idyllic society,,, when apparently none exists.

When one pulls back, giving up on the dream and the illusions,,, does one see the atrocities of that society more clearly. Only with time and exposure to the light of intelligence and reasoning, do we discover each system within each system that has its devastating flaws,,, and I would add, are or have within all **Parasitical Societies**.

The characteristics of each system (and there are many) or society are much the same, regardless of its origin. There are patterns that each follow, they fall into much the same dysfunction as Scrupulosity. This is a man-made mental disorder found within most all religions.

Any one society is made up of many overlapping societies (boxes) that are divided into many divisions. Those boxes or walls become insurmountable regardless of which side you are standing on. This wall building is passed on from parent to child and the dysfunction process that I call Socialosity,,, continues. Even if you have lived within one society all of your life you can be isolated, due to your gender, skin color, the fact that you are left-handed, your hair, your height, your weight, your religion or lack thereof and so on.

Recognizing the dysfunction within you is half way to fixing it.

Now that you see it,,,
Remove it!!!

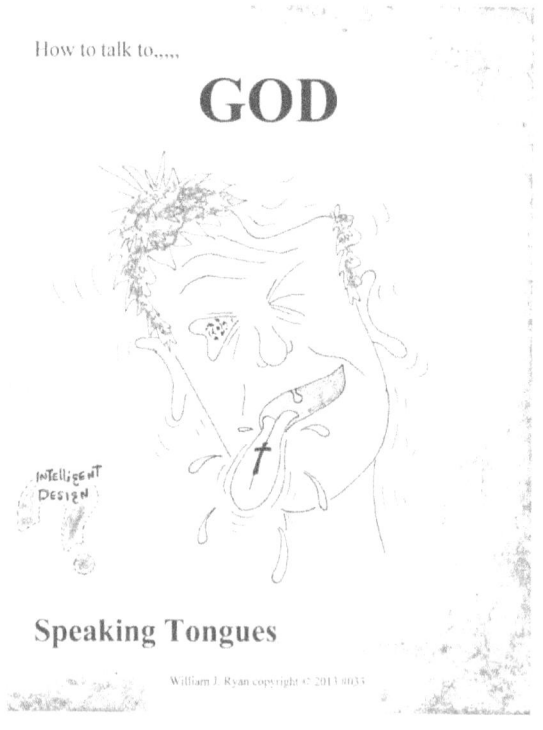

How to talk to,,,,,

GOD

INTELLIGENT DESIGN

Speaking Tongues

William J. Ryan copyright © 2013

The face of one near you speaking rubbish,,, poisoning your mind for control over you and your money.

Examples of society dysfunctions are so numerous, that its origins can be found inside each of us. We create a society within our individual homes and pass that on to our children and they in turn pass it on to theirs. Bigotries and hatred have their roots in our homes and are given to each of us at an early age, so we carry them all of our lives, passing them on when and where we can.

These become monsters that grow into tribes and then cultures and societies, the worst being religions that lead us into endless wars, killing each other to defend our beliefs. Regardless of the sheer magnitude of the insanity (lies) found within. The spirit, too weak to stand up to these glaring lies within religions is the prime example of **Socialosity**. The strong desire to want to *belong to something,,, anything*, makes people look the other way in order to keep from being alone. Being alone is not so bad, sometimes life is better when you get all the nut jobs out of your life and away from your newly cleaned and healthy brain.

Examples of dysfunction placed in trust within a society;

1. **Politician** (Poli-Christians); above the laws made for the rest of us. *"We make our own laws for us."*
2. **Law Enforcement**; twisting the laws to benefit them. *"We choose which laws we will enforce."*
3. **Attorneys**; an art form of lying. *Some think Caesar of the Roman Empire said it best, "The first thing we should do is kill all the attorneys."* Another example of bias passed on.

31

4. **Doctors**; self-enrichment,,, keep your patient sick by prescribing medication they don't need, so they have to keep coming back. *That is until their bank account is empty.*

5. **Bankers**; the art of taking money. *They don't make money,,, they take money and I would add, as much as they can carry,,, legally or illegally.*

6. **Governments**; masters of open deception. *Laws designed to enrich the chosen ones.* ***See the second constitution of 1871 and THE UNITED STATES OF AMERICA INCORPORATED COMPANY 1925.***

7. **Countries**; wars, killing over god. *America, the most destabilizing **FAKE** country in the world, openly spreads it lies to the masses, using religion and they, the faithful, gobble them up (the lies) like it were candy for the soul, blindly without question. Sometimes this is called blind faith.*

8. **Religion and Priests**; raping children without punishment. *The Pope,,, standing next to God himself,,, protects pedophiles,,, and the masses,,, **2.5 billion** people follow him and hang on his every word. **The truth is the pope stands next to the Sun God Satan and sex with a child is a Rite Of Passage,,, a requirement!!!***

9. **Educators**; teaching the art of deception. *Anything for a buck is passed on within the Jesuit as they will do anything,,, kill anyone so as to get the gold. **"Make and wage relentless war"** for it matters not who should suffer,,, only that they should control through their god,,, Satan.*

    The dominant force behind all these societies,,, interwoven within, is race, gender, religion and all its prejudices, hatreds and bigotries. Most times, the Parasitical Religion is at the core. Used as the catalyst to justify the lies and brutalities by the many **Deceivers** around us. Their thinking is, *'You back my lie and I will back yours and each of us will get rich taking advantage of the ignorant,'* *thereby, mastering the art of deception.*

The parallels of each system of society,,, the evils,,, the atrocities committed within one society over another are often justified. These religious cults stick together like one would imagine and whitewash the crimes, covering them up (Pope/pedophiles). Their thinking is, *'It is ok to kill,,, rape,,, plunder (the spoils of war) if you are killing for god,,, for Satan.'*

This should bother you if you didn't know that. And yes, there is something you can do!

Examples of religions that kill for god:
1. Judaism
2. Christianity/Catholicism
3. Muslim
4. Islam
5. Buddhist

And the list of religions goes on to cover most, if not all.

What I discovered after writing the book Scrupulosity,,, the madness found within all religions,,, is that this man made insanity extends into every aspect of every culture. Until we recognize the dysfunctions all around us, we cannot ever begin to repair them. We cannot ever stop this madness and move forward within a global society without Scrupulosity and Socialosity, if we don't stop,,, look at it,,, and try to find the truth.

Socialosity

It is there in front of us,,, but you must look, giving up your Blind Faith. You must try to see the part that **you** play within these many overlapping societies. We all are knee deep in the **SCAT** of these **Predator Parasites** that feed upon all of us and thrive on our ignorance. These manmade societies are controlled by them, the few, the rich,,, the aristocratic.

Understanding **Socialosity** is the first step out of their waste. Where one can rise above it and for the first time for some, breathe the clean healthy air just above. This act of self-awareness will lift you up and free you from their clutches and the evil within.

All of these lies are a poison within our physical body, destroying us from within, as our true self tries to get out, knowing in ones higher self, the difference from right and wrong. *The black oozing sores within our souls,,, placed there by others,,, can began to be healed.*

Example;
1. A priest **raping a child** and the church,,, the religion pays hush money to cover it all up in order to make it go away.
2. The 6th commandment of their god is: **"Thou shalt not kill."** Yet, the Christian crusades killed millions and still are to this very day as the **religious** look the other way.

How can one remain a Christian when you know this to be true? These truths eat at your soul and the virus,,, the lies,,, this parasite called religion destroys you from within. Suicide rates are very high within the society of the American Veterans and it all gets swept under the rug. Let's all pretend there is not a problem. The problem has a name and that name is **Socialosity** and its 4 levels.

One thing that might be helping to push our Vets over the edge could be the discovery that the 9/11 attack on the World Trade Center was a GREAT HOAX upon the American people. Millions of people have died in this "relentless war" that's enriching the few. Benjamin Netanyahu said it best,,, "This is a good thing (9/11) for Israel." Israel warned its people (Jews) to stay away from the World Trade Center that morning. Look up; The Dancing Israelis that set up cameras to document the "dustification of the towers.

One report shows

Vets make up 7 percent of the American population but account for 20 percent of its suicides

"An alarming rise"

Socialosity

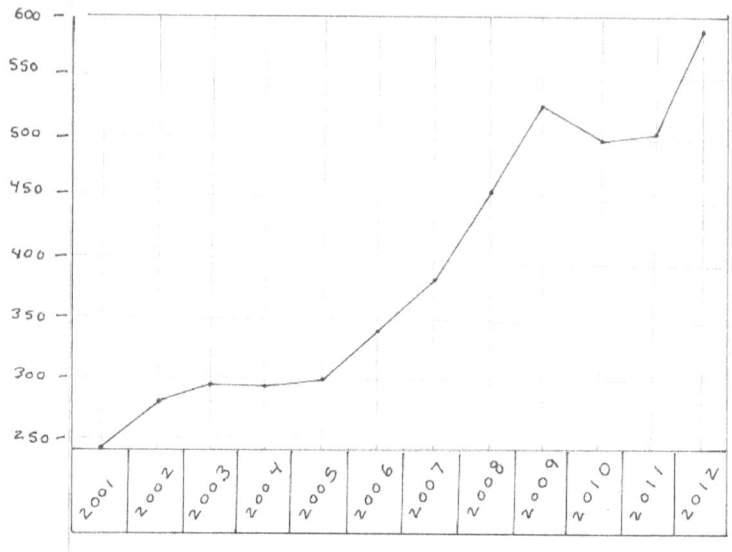

Many of the World War Two German high ranking children committed suicide because of what their fathers had done in the war.

Chapter Three

Manufactured People

A comical view (from the 1930s) of what most men at that time would think of women and their makeup

This is extremely difficult for me to write,,, but I will push through.

Vanity and all of its levels is something we are all born with. We spend a lifetime endearing, cultivating, selling or manipulating others for the purpose of positioning ourselves in a higher class within one of these societies. This is the one thread (like the need for god or the old man in the sky) that is truly woven throughout each race as beauty rises to the top, (like evil) searching for the money and power it brings over others.

It would seem to start at birth for each one of us, when we inherit that precious **DNA.** We fall into those classifications (those boxes) that determine our position for the rest of our life. It is those classifications that are passed on from one generation to another, many times by culture, religion and beyond any one society.

Each one of us falls into those categories (those boxes), we are meant to believe,,, set by god himself for are we all not made in his image? Therein, we become what we are told will be our future by those that must know. If your father was a stone cutter,,, you will become a stone cutter. If your father was a baker,,, you will become a baker and so on. Many of our last names were given to us by our previous positions. However, how you look to others can break you free of that forced society.

Additionally each of these boxes was created by one race or another. For all of their life; they must endure or overcome these limitations set by others. One such glaring example of such a classification at birth is the La Casta.

Now do bear in mind the fact that I did not make this up. The Roman Catholic Church did in the 17th and the 18th centuries.

At this time the satanic Jesuits had taken over the Roman Catholic Church in the late 16th century and they wanted to destroy the heretics.

"and I will spare neither age, sex or condition; and that I will hang, waste, boil, flay, strangle and bury alive these infamous heretics, rip up the stomachs and wombs of their women and crush their infants heads against the wall, in order to annihilate forever their execrable race."

This should bother you,,,
If it does not,,,
You should be asking why.

La Casta

Beauty then will rise to the top within each one of these La Casta skin color rating classifications. Vanity then takes over as the most beautiful children learn and become the privileged and those of less or without beauty or with defects; fall to lower positions within **each** overlapping society.

This each person knows from personal experience starting at childhood and I would add, they each carry them to their deaths with their attitudes of superiorly. These ratings are forced upon us by the bullies in our lives. We each have had a deep personal experience with every aspect of these rating's by the time we reach maturity.

Maturity, for some can be found at an early age. Many times it is believed to be brought into this life from the very old souls. For others, they never seem to reach maturity, struggling for a lifetime with unattainable,,, beauty. Others find it a curse and withdraw into themselves.

Vanity Level One

Each one of us possess the skills to rate every person on the planet and we do so without **conscious** hesitation, instantaneously. Deep within the human mind are these classification abilities, which are a very old series of recordings, perhaps within our **DNA**. When we first encounter another person coming towards us, our **automatic** UNCONSCIOUS reaction is to think,,,

1. Is this male or female, a man or a woman?
2. Are they attractive,,, sexually?

Each one of us does this automatically, for it is what we are deep inside. For most of us it is so much part of our nature,,, our inner core,,, that we don't even notice it when it happens. Rating others is just part of what we are or have become taught by others. Regardless of where we land on this planet,,, we all do the same thing,,, rate others. This one ability is present within all societies,,, not just the Roman Catholic church. It is therefore something I believe we bring with us into this life,,, the quest for beauty,,, acceptance,,, desire,,, love from others. A common thread of *Socialosity found* in each of us that now can be seen with more clarity. That understanding would also extend to all forms of life including, **Koko the gorilla**. Understand that vanity fact, helps each one of us to become kinder,,, but we will never stop rating others and putting them in a box,,, never. We can't because we (our souls) are all in physical bodies that sexually reproduce.

I would like to add that I believe we look at the true aura of the soul when on the other side. If it is of a desired color,,, we are drawn,,, if of an unwanted color we pull away. This soul aura, we carry with us into this short life.

Vanity Level Two

By the reaction of others, (long desired stares) the chosen ones grow to believe them, that somehow they are special and deserving of better treatment than those not as beautiful. A temporary gift from our inherited **DNA** meant only to attract the opposite sex, for the purpose of breeding; has moved those perceived chosen ones above the rest of us normal looking people for a very short time.

For these perceived pretty people, they become possessed,,, fascinated with their own looks of desirability. They spend too much time studying their own reflection of their face in the mirror, imprisoned within their own vanity, believing they are better than the rest of us. They are fascinated with trying to achieve greater perfection. The mirror is the worst invention man has ever made, for it (like the La Casta) has created an even larger temporary rift between each one of us. More walls that divide us, within each of our societies, as beauty and its temporary privileges are the ultimate goal for all of us, regardless of our age.

This temporary division, walls or boxes, sometimes can last a lifetime, as desires to remain beautiful and attractive and those special perks that come with beauty, possess the soul until the grave. For those pulled into the societal cult of beauty, they enter a whole new level of *Socialosity*.

Vanity Level Three

At this level beauty can become a curse and for those women possessing beauty, fending off men's attractions becomes a daily chore. I have heard (more than once the words), **"I wish I was not so pretty."** You can see them struggle with it in their minds as they push people away with their eyes,,, and yet they cover their faces in paint meant to attract; clearly, **an oxymoron (they don't want it but they do) among society classifications**.

It should be noted that when men possess beauty or handsomeness,,, they see it as a blessing. When women are attracted to them for their looks they take them to bed and dump them the next day. It would seem, women use their looks to get money and men use their looks to get sex.

For those who enjoy the comments, looks, stares, and attractions, they just can't get enough of it. They start to peruse help with their physical changes making them more desirable. These people are what I call,,, **The Manufactured People**.

This part of **Level Three** I have firsthand experience with, for I dated such a woman. Men would chase her home and she would have to call the police. One man ran up to her car window and ejaculated on the car glass.

She was torn between the desire to make herself beautiful and its curse. Because of my history in dealing with the public, I have firsthand experience and am all too familiar with people and their mental disorders. I have read many books that helped me read people's expressions and body language that helped me with sales.

After years of dealing with the public, I gained a keen insight into reading their thoughts and emotions. Following a truly beautiful and vain person into a department store is an experience I never want to relive. It was that horrendous of a day and it goes against every fiber of my being. This is the worst stage of **Vanity Level Three** that I have ever personally experienced.

As we were spending time together and I let her drag me to a mall,,, **big mistake**. We went clothes shopping,,, shoe shopping,,, and then the worst thing imaginable,,, makeup. *"Oh god what have I done to myself?"* I think I am going to be sick just remembering this and reliving it. I have suppressed it for a very long time,,, keeping the memories in my black ooze bag filled with nightmares.

I followed her like a puppy, into a room that looked like a cathedral designated to please the gods of beauty. There was total reverence, silence as each woman there was entranced in the possibilities of achieving their goal,,, total beauty,,, well beyond pretty. Each woman was in a slow motion trance,,, hypnotized by the thought that they too could cross the line of normal to super human,,, supper beauty,, all desirable,,, above the masses.

Mesmerized,,, I watched my friend move very slowly from counter to counter, touching each item as though by doing so,,, perfection would appear and carry her to a new level of desirability. The longer I stood there watching these women at this level of vanity, the sicker I was becoming.

As though the vibrations coming from this place,,, from these women was some sort of poison, killing me,,, burning a hole in my soul.

Their intense stares at each and every item, every color, every scent, I could hear their minds thinking, *'Maybe green is my color,,, or red,,, or yellow,,, or purple or....'* The vanity sounds and vibrations were becoming deafening as this society of the ravenous females searched for what was not ever to be. They tried every magic potion or elixir on display. I could see that it showed deeply upon their faces,,, **'Maybe the next one,,, I must keep looking.'**

The young woman behind the counter tried not to look up at any of the **Non Pretty People** that were trying to obtain what they would never possess, the illusion of beauty that they were selling. This counter woman was stunning, clearly hired for her looks,,, (not her sales ability or people skills) looked down her nose at everyone else as though she and only she possessed the power of beauty, the **Key Master**. She was the keeper of the keys and when she saw my friend,,, who I will call L,,, she approached her with her eyes open,,, smiling. I could read her mind, **'Oh here is one like me.'** One at her level, within (her box), that she could truly relate to, speaking the same language of the desired ones.

By this point, I was becoming sick to my stomach at the **waves of intense vanity** coming from the room and these desperate entranced females. I knew **L** had two large fishing tackle boxes full of different color make up that she has never used and here we are, trying to buy more. The hypocrisy of vanity was ripping at my soul. I needed to pull away from this place and its intense waves of nauseating vibrations.

To me, this is clearly a sickness of the human mind,,, for this woman, **L**, was cursed with beauty and the unwanted attractions of men,,, yet there she was,,, standing before the alter of the almighty,,, the holiest of hollies,,, entranced with the hope of finding the elusive scepter of almighty beauty. *I was about to throw up.* I could stand it no more, so I told her I had to leave.

She said,,, "No wait,,, I am almost done."

Once more I told her more intently. I was getting sick and I had to leave this place. Perhaps it was all of the smells, but I think deep in my heart,,, deep in my soul,,, it was the intense vanity that was driving me away like a bulldozer,,, oil and water,,, never mixing. Finally,

I rose my voice,,, "I am getting sick,,, I am leaving now," and as I walked outside, she followed me, most puzzled.

Once outdoors I leaned on a pillar and tried to breath in clean air, away from all the products of vanity and their sickening fragrances. There,,, free of the intense waves of narcissism, conceit, self-love, self-admiration, self-absorption my soul was fully returning to the body.

It was truly one of the most horrendous experiences of my life and I will never go into such a life threatening place again. The intense waves of vanity seemed to emanate from every item, every product; even the walls and floor. Exposure to all those waves of vanity coming from all those women at the same time was like Kryptonite to Superman. I am no superman, but I know the intense feeling of death he must have felt, weakened and sickened by such an intense power.

At that time, I could not put into words what I just described in writing. **L** did not understand and I tried to explain it to her but could not. She saw nothing wrong,,, and that was the sad part,,, for this is the essence of **Socialosity**,,, blindness to ones actions.

Level Three Vanity is the reason malls have benches outside stores. A place for men to sit,,, safe from the **Vanity Kryptonite** that will kill them with prolonged exposure.

I truly believe that I could watch a man eat a baby alive, before I could witness the intense vanity that I experienced, which caused me to crumble in its wake that day.

Man Eating New Born Baby

*The worst part of writing this book was writing that memory, detailing the **Socialosity of Vanity** at the 3rd level. I dreaded it so intensely.*

I truly don't expect most women to understand, but I do believe that most men would get it. The clashes of these two societies, male and female, grow ever deeper with this vanity rift between us. The next level is when vanity is used like a weapon,,, a tool for extraction and destruction.

Vanity Level Four

Each one of our species (humans),,, male and female, wallow within deferring levels of vanity. Most times it becomes destructive on many personal levels.

Looking (from the outside) at the human race,,, (a race to what I am not sure,,, most likely the end of the human race) we have evolved into a mass of self-indulgent beings, (the I or me people). Vanity would seem to be a trait we all bring with us at birth. We believe we are beautiful and perhaps that is a true reflection of our soul not our physical bodies. At birth most of us are beautiful and later in life we become grotesque and repulsive.

Evil always rises to the top of everything,,, religion, government and business. Vanity does much the same and in this level of **Socialosity** it takes many strange, bazaar and destructive actions. In this **Level Four of Vanity,** I have had to break it down into several sections that encompass men and women and their divisions in this part of **Socialosity**.

Makeup

Face paint (or war paint) to most of us, has reached new levels of **vanity** never seen before. With these new levels of usage of these virtually **unregulated products,** women have seen an increase of **FACIAL CANCER**. There are many reports of these **harsh chemicals that cause cancer** and yet women line up,,, mesmerized,,, to buy them knowing the risks.

One such report estimates **the average woman put over 160 chemicals on their body every day,,, EVERY DAY!** The need to experiment on the human body,,, the immune system,,, the long term **damage to our DNA is passed on to our children**.

Women and men can find all manner of means to change their perceived flaws. Some women,,, I have heard of,,, are inherently lazy and not willing to dedicate the time at the vanity table (or the goo table) each day to,,, **putting on their faces**,,, so they have them **tattooed on**.

Yes, I said **tattooed on**, so each morning they are ready to go out into public possessing their self-perceived beauty,,, without all the work. *Now stop and think of what I just said.*

The only thing is, when the swelling and infection goes down,,, they look like clowns and it is permanent. Now they must cover their face with makeup to cover the intense inks that have been used to dye their skin,,, permanently. The *Socialosity* **Level Four** insanity of **Vanity** is clear in this example of damage.

Vanity is a powerful unseen force that drives us all,,, it pushes us to do many things and we permit it to take over our lives. It can ultimately destroy us, like a cancer,,, eating our soul from within. Recognizing the different levels can only help us **not** make life altering irreversible destructive mistakes.

To me, as a writer and an artist, I look at everything, to try to discover all aspects and all sides. I immerse myself into both sides of any given situation for viewpoints and understanding from all sides. I prosecute and defend a point of view. To help make my point, I would like to use the face from my book *Adina of Elysium*.

Adina is a young female from the 12th century, before the need of perfection to make something of our face that is not real in order to cover up the real person underneath. A mask of deception that must be worn at all times to cover the self-perceived hideousness underneath,,, or the real you that must be hidden.

When I look at Adina I see the innocence of her young age, as she presents only her true self in this looking glass,,, mirror-less society. Before a time when it became necessary to mask our true self, pretending to be something we are not and *somehow that became ok.*

As I understand it, face makeup started in France and was believed by many outside that country to be repulsive. Something only a whore would wear when wanting sex.

Before a life where the newly created walls of **Socialosity Vanity**, divided all of us and neatly placed each one of us in a box according to how our face looks to others. The power of perception and perfection over the soul and spirit is very destructive for all sides.

No one is to see the inner beauty of our soul shining through,,, rising to the top like a beacon in the fog of life, emanating acceptance from one soul to another. Instead we see the **Socialosity,,, Mask of Vanity**, covering the perceived physical flaws. A man made disorder, that reveals a hideous monster created just under the surface. The more makeup, the deeper the **vanity** scars beneath and the more it pushes normal people away. Perhaps that is the goal, for they (the immature) want only to be part of the elusive and exclusive club of the beautiful,,, as they perceive it.

In creating an image of Adina I wanted a normal child's face. Almost all young people are attractive to a point and Adina must possess those childlike qualities as well as the beginnings of a young woman. Most importantly she must appear to be normal.

There is a fine line between pretty and beautiful and I tried to build that within her face,,, attractive,,, but not beautiful. Beauty is something men want to own and are willing to kill to get it. She must not possess the destructive beauty.

Adina of Elysium

Please notice this image of Adina is that of a young girl, without makeup on her face. To me the forms of the human face are attractive in and of themselves. They need nothing and should never be covered up. The act of concealing ones true self is in itself a destructive act and reflective of a damaged soul within the body, pursuing some type of perfection.

*The damage of **Socialosity** is in every society on this planet and is passed on from one generation to another. For many of us, we are taught that **"God made man in his image"**,,, so (per the religious) we all look like god,,, and the human body must be covered up at all times. That would make God himself,,, hideous,,, right?*

Adina's image is a fictional creation of mine from the twelfth century (before wide spread face paint) and I believe to most people her face is attractive. But move her into the 21st century and up the scale of vanity. There are many hideous examples of deformities that must be hidden,,, covered up,,, altered,,, so as to conceal her real self, her true glow that is a reflection of her true soul just beneath.

In the 21st century Adina would be given these modern social abnormalities (walls and boxes) from others well trained in the art of pointing out every flaw and then covering it up. She would be transformed from feeling good about herself as a human being to feeling bad because every flaw,,, every hideous imperfection has been pointed out to her. So, now she must hide her troll like deformities.

Adina lives in a time before each and every perceived hideous imperfection must be surgically altered, covered up and concealed under gallons of unapproachable goo, as she is shown how to create her mask of deception or manmade manufactured beauty. This act alone reveals weakness in their mental state that they were taught by others,,, the act of self-destructive **vanity** and a life of trying to reach the unattainable. Adina's life is to be free of this man made disorder of **Socialosity,,, Vanity**.

I believe when a normal man looks at Adina's face, he sees a young attractive female. Most all young men and women at this age are attractive and need nothing. However, when a young woman of today looks at the face of Adina, they see thousands of imperfections that must be covered up. The disorder of vanity is taught and passed on from mother to her female child.

I am sure they can start with Adina's ears. I deliberately made them different lengths,,, uneven, so she would not be perfect. As are her eyebrows, her chin, nose, eyes and her lips,,, all off center just a bit. Today, she would be considered a train wreck; required to undergo many years of reconstructive surgery and years of intense training in the art of,,, **putting on her mask** to cover her hideous face.

This man made disorder or Society of **Vanity**, has grown and infects every female child. This virus can reveal every imperfection, destroying the self-worth of the being,,, the soul,,, child within. The lifetime damage is done and passed on from generation to generation.

Surgery

Why people see only the flaws in ones face falls at the feet of the people that want to make money (or take money) selling remedies, potions and elixirs to all the imperfect people that they can find,,, or create. Trust me, they will find them all and have a product to sell them. With Adina's face, she will need to have her ears trimmed to balance out her face and her lips adjusted to position them in the center where perfection can be obtained.

The risk of surgery, infection, bad surgeons mistakes,,, by taking off to much or not enough and all the days, weeks, months of recovery,,, in a normal mind,,, just can't be worth it. But to some women and men,,, trained in vanity, perfection is ($$$), this can only be the true goal and remedy.

The perceived opinions of others are so vital, that it would push them to make the changes. The risk to them is small and the gains so great to have temporary beauty and the longing stares of acceptance at a new level. This thinking is most foreign and bazaar to me. I will never understand, especially knowing all the things that can go wrong,,, the risks.

True Story,,, Female Nose Job;

A woman felt her nose was too stumpy and she **paid** to have a plastic surgeon remove part of one of her earlobes and put it on the end of her nose. **This is a true story!** Now stop and think,,, what kind of a vain idiot would do such a thing? The answer is, someone suffering from the sickness of **Socialosity Vanity**. Nonetheless, she did it and when the bandages were removed,,, guess what,,, she looked like she had an earlobe on the end of her nose.

Surgery to change our appearance and fix our perceived imperfections is not just a female social disorder, for men also have fallen ill under the sickness of **Social Vanity**. It has been reported that Michael Jackson had many surgeries to change his appearance and over the years of his life, one can see all the changes slowly reveal themselves as his face changes.

True Story,,, Male Nose Job;

A man wanted a more roman nose and perfection was the motive as **Social Vanity** took over his life. So, he underwent plastic surgery and when the Band-Aids came off,,, so did his nose. He looked like the Phantom of the Opera,,, living in a sewer underground,,, when his white mask was removed.

After the infection went down, he could have a second surgery to replace flesh that could be shaped later and that one was a success,,, (if you can call it that). Think of the pain this man endured at the hands of **Social Vanity**. His dreams of joining the social elite, the beautiful manufactured people,,, dashed forever.

The plastic surgeon was able to graft a hunk of his fore arm to his face. He had to have his arm held to his head for weeks until the transformation could be complete. When the arm was removed,,, there was a hunk of flesh hanging from the center of his face that made him look like he had a sausage coming out of his head. The insane price of vanity people are willing to pay,,, mesmerizing.

The action of the surgeon that took their money, feeding off their **Vanity**, is but one form of **Level Four.** As you will see, it takes on many faces. Liposuction is another form of extracting money from the vain. There are many more stories, some which even include death.

Chapter Four

The Goal

The Ultimate Goal

Perfection in beauty as I understand makes the possessor feel good and is the ultimate goal, which unseats jealousy and envy,,, both very destructive forces that can manifest themselves within **Level Four of Vanity**. Look closely and you will see the anger in their (the possessors) eyes,,, as they grow closer to the perceived perfection they all seek. *I personally believe this anger is due to their finding themselves in a world filled with trolls and hideous creatures,,, or as the rest of us would call normal people and their flaws.*

This combined energy (jealousy and envy) can take on a life of its own. The pretense of this other person,,, this mask that has been put on each day, becomes who we project to others,,, our self-perceived image.

This temporary image replaces our soul, covering it and all its true beauty or evil just under the skin. For some, it takes over their lives. This may be hard to believe, but some women even wear makeup to bed,,, bazaar,,, but true. Their quest to hold and maintain temporary beauty,,, even in their sleep.

I speak from personal experience on this one, for I dated a woman that I found attractive (not beautiful) and apparently, because she had red hair she had hardly any eyebrows. I did not know, because I did not look and did not care,,, for it mattered not.

She did not wear a lot of makeup (one reason I found her attractive,,, she was real not fake), but sometime within our discovery of each other, I found she painted on her eye brows. Mistakenly in play sometime later I rubbed them off, discovering her real self, her real beauty.

To me it mattered not, I only wanted to show that I did not care, wanting only to see her true self,,, and I did. She became quite upset and had to replace the painted on eyebrows, completing the look she wanted to project before going to sleep.

Her damaged soul and vanity pushed her to put on paint completing the mask, the illusion and then she could go to bed. It was very bazaar!!! I never understood and I still don't,,, or maybe deep down I do. She is covering up a physical flaw pointed out to her by the other catty females from her past, which is now deeply ingrained into her being,,, her damaged soul.

Strange as this might sound, I just wanted to know her better and be closer to her, showing her I did not care about this image, the mask. But she threw this wall up between us,,, among many others,,, and it would seem we were doomed. Her sickness of **vanity** and the social club she was trying to join or remain within was but one of many unseen walls between us.

It is obvious that she had been damaged and herself worth was so low, so beaten down, that this in her mind helped her feel better about herself. But there are other examples I know of where the man,,, a shallow man,,, insisted on the woman dressing in her full makeup every day,,, every morning just as she got out of bed. That's the complete opposite of me and confusing to understand their attraction to the image and not the real person.

Realizing there were two opposite ends of this spectrum, (two societies of thought) I dug into this more deeply and discovered that there are mothers teaching their female children how to put on makeup at a very early age. But there is not just the art of creating a new face,,, a mask to hide behind,,, a new image to project to others,,, but they also teach their prejudices,,, passing on the damage,,, their damage,,, to the young.

The art of **Landing A Man,,,** a rich man is another part of this teaching. Apparently, the more makeup, the greater the level of beauty is perceived.

With that comes the programming,,, *"Don't make the same mistakes I did."* or *"First time for love and second time for money is not for you,,, you go for money first."* and it is then I noticed the deep anger.

Over centuries of time, I could see a pretty young girl like Adina, start to cover her face with goo and she would began to push people away,,, all the people that were poor or not beautiful. Each would attempt to make themselves more attractive to the opposite sex, becoming more pretentious and angrier with every passing day.

This anger stems from being surrounded by the ugly and not getting want they want all the time, because they are in the special class of the perceived beautiful,,, therefore very special and deserving.

This need to attract only the superior, forced them to practice the art of makeup more intently; all the while searching in vain for the (deserved) doctors, attorneys or a rich man's son, pushing away all other unqualified suitors. Their failing is clearly only in their **Gold Digging** minds. Not the type of makeup or how they apply it,,, but the money,,, as their mothers and their stuck up friends taught them.

For these rich young men, the aphrodisiac of money is clearly strong and when wealth is exposed to these young women, they open up and give it all up. They (rich young men) use them like an endless supply of tissues from a box. Good looking men know this as well. I witnessed two of them in action in my lifetime.

The rich could be fat, ugly and a creep, but it did not matter. For the money,,, dads money,,, was the draw that pulled them all in towards the fire, where each would surely be burned. Ninety-nine out of a hundred times, they usually were.

The really good looking men had experienced the same thing. These shallow pretentious young women would throw themselves at them if they (the man) said or did the right things. They (the good looking man) just had to stand still and wait and they would come.

First, they sometimes had to pretend to be rich,,, both these cases of good looking men were poor, had tax liens and in bankruptcy at one time, forever bouncing off the bottom of life. It seemed each week they would come to work with another stunning woman on their arm that they picked up in a bar. That week they would nail her and then dump her and the next week and it would start all over again.

They took great pleasure in obtaining their goal of sex with these pretentious, phony, plastic, **Gold Digging** women and then dumping them. Like a tee-shirt collection or trophies on a wall, only they stopped keeping track of them, because there were so many. Sometimes not even remembering who they were from month to month when they would come back, drugs and alcohol will help do that. One had a collection of phone numbers on his desk and I asked him who they were and he said, "Girls I met, I just don't remember their names." There were dozens of numbers on small pieces of paper in piles.

The point is,,, every good looking man I ever met did the same thing,,, used the aphrodisiac of the pretense of money and their good looks to take advantage of the narcissism that is deeply ingrained in all of these pretentious women (there were so many). For the rest of us, these women are easy to spot, for they were all dressed to the nines,,, covered in tons of makeup and full of anger. One time I asked one, *"If I throw you against the wall would you stick?"* in front of her date and he laughed as he drug her out the door on their first and last date. I could do that because she is just another victim of her self-destructive narcissistic **vanity.** It just did not matter, for the next day he would bring another.

After years of failing to find the rich man of their dreams,,, or their mothers dreams,,, they find new ways to get the cash. I don't mean the kind of prostitution found on the street, but a different kind of prostitution found in the courts.

Sexual Harassment

As the art of makeup is learned and passed on to their young,,, within the female society and with all the narcissistic disappointments of the self-diagnosed, pretty but not beautiful mother,,, they seem to move collectively to a new level of hate and anger towards all men. *ME TOO!!!* Their frustration of not getting their hands on the cash, (someone else's cash) is compounded by the inability to land the right one (money) in their life and that anger is passed on. *"I wasted my youth,,, my best years on you!"*

Their disappointment turns to anger and is revealed upon their faces even as they walk alone. It can be spotted if one will just take the time to look. Peoples thoughts are revealed within each expression and as they replay the mothers words over and over in their minds,,, old recordings,,, feelings,,, accompanied thoughts,,, frustration is revealed.

You have to look and you will see the anger. As they get older, they don't even try to hide it anymore. I believe that in today's Meat Market, these young women think their anger makes them look more attractive,,, but it is not working. *Or it is to push away any and all suitors that don't meet her perceived concept of money or looks. They have to meet the minimum requirements (of her Social Click) before one can even be talking to her.*

The art of using their looks to get what they want, has failed to land them the doctor or attorney they wanted (or their mother wanted). Now they are stuck with the losers. This in fact, may be the source of the anger. Children hear fights and these words, ***"I could have married XXX!"*** The disappointment is then passed on to the next generation and the cycle continues.

At this young adult stage in their lives, they will do anything to anyone, if it will make them money. The art of making themselves so attractive to men takes a new turn. With the biggest of smiles, turning their flirtation on high, like sharks to blood and raw meat, they move in for the kill.

The innocent man can't tell the difference between harmless flirtation and the desire to just have sex with him. To most men,,, ***"It's just sex"*** (probably because men don't have to carry the baby), but to a woman it is an understandable lifetime commitment,,, and a way to get the money. *After some time, one can spot the Gold Diggers quickly. When one would approach me, I* *would just tell them "I don't have any money" (even though I do) and they would just walk away.*

The aphrodisiac of money they can't have, after turning on all their charms, once more gets put to the flames. Only this time it is revenge they seek against all men. Their misconstrued, over flirtatious actions are too much to resist (by the man) or misinterpreted, then POW,,, BANG,,, the cash register is opened and complaints are filed. Attorneys are called and the EEOC gets involved,,, classes are taught as to how to treat women in the workplace. We see it coming in full bloom today, as **The Me Too Society** grows.

As of today, the accusations are flying about and the list of big money men (not poor) being attacked is growing every day. The campaign,,, the **Socialosity** of revenge has created the **ME TOO** campaign. Rightly or wrongly accused,,, the accusations will bring down the strongest of men.

They are titans in their industry. If one of these women should be a deranged narcissistic liar, hell bent upon revenge against a man (any man will do as long as they are rich), that rejected her years ago,,, what better way to get even **and get the money**. Add your name to the **Me Too** campaign and get the cash.

Men,,, all men are learning to just back away, keep to yourself, give up on the family concept of the 50s and don't have kids. Better to have them sign a dating contract.

Disclaimer

*The following list of names reflects only those in the public eye (all rich) who have **allegedly** been accused of sexual misconduct. Some claims are over **40 years old**. To wait so long suggests only that this is not about justice,,, but about **money**.*

We should all try to remember,,, they are all <u>*innocent until proven guilty*</u> *in a court of law.*

Like the POPE (a man standing next to god) said, "Show me the proof," to the child rape victims of the Roman Catholic Church. Otherwise they are all committing "<u>Slander</u>"

This is the (Jesuit) pope that said that!

As of December 27th 2017, the list of (rich) accused is very long and allegedly included people like;

1. President John F. Kennedy
2. President Bill Clinton
3. President Donald J. Trump; *One of the accusers of sexual misconduct said, "He kissed me and I am damaged for life." In some (metropolitan) cultures,,, some societies,,, kissing is a greeting. I cannot believe a kiss would destroy a life,,, unless it was said by her to try to get to the money. Why else repeat it publicly, knowing how lecherous it makes her look to others?*
4. Bill Cosby: *Reported; case ended in a mistrial as of 06/17/17,,, second trial Bill was sentenced to 3 to 10 years. What a loss for all of us,,, and now we see how vanity can rule one's life.*
5. Harvey Weinstein
6. Charlie Rose
7. Dustin Hoffman; *It should be noted that one of the news aired photos of Mr. Hoffman, showed*

him being groped by a female. *The image broadcast showed his sex organs being grabbed by her as she was smiling for the photo. How can she claim sexual harassment when it looks like it was* **consensual**? *To some, this starts to look like envy, jealousy and revenge for them not getting his money,,, marriage.*

8. Matt Lauer
9. Roy Moor
10. Al Franken
11. Joe Barton
12. John Conyers
13. Trent Franks
14. Mario Batali

And on and on and on it goes.

This recent wave of ghost's from the past coming forward can only serve the belief that this is only about the money. If one of these **men** *stood up and fought their accusers,,, in court,,, Slander, Defamation,,, this madness (these ghost from the past) would most likely end. But it takes one* **man** *to do that,,, a man.*

These present day examples only help me show our future as a split society divided by our gender. The social rift between men and women is becoming so great that workplace romance is becoming a thing of the past.

'My job is more important than love, so I will not risk it. Besides I don't know if I say anything like, *"Would you like to have lunch,"* would that be misconstrued as *"Would you like to have sex"* so better to say nothing.'

Each of us then learn the art of masturbation and lose the joy of shared love making or sweaty animal games, as this **modern man made rift of Socialosity** between the sexes grows ever larger.

Damage done by the accused in this stage, **Level Four**, is irreversible. Like accusing a man of child molestation,,, the words can't be undone. The lure of beauty has a very powerful effect upon people. In this next example it is revealed to just what extent **Socialosity** has turned.

One such example is Debra L (no last names in order to protect identity), a young female teacher in a Middle School in Florida. She pleaded guilty in 2005 to lewd or lascivious battery against a 14 year old boy. Her attorney John F. argued that Debra is…

"Too pretty for prison," thereby setting a precedence that all pretty women can rape boys without penalty.

For her crimes it was reported she received NO prison time from the sitting judge on the case,,, *sending a clear message to all*. In 2014 the **Florida Supreme Court** (perhaps captivated by her beauty) ruled in favor of Debra and her appeal to end her probation,,, *as though it never happened. And it is done,,, there are two types of justice for the same crime depending if you are a man or a woman*.

Beauty is so ingrained within all of our societies that crimes committed against children,,, by the pretty female people,,, can go without punishment,,, jail time. If she were fat and covered with tattoos or scars,,, looking the commonly perceived part of a convict,,, (not pretty) would she have then gone to jail? If she were a man having plead guilty to lewd and lascivious battery on a

14 year old girl, he would still be in prison,,, pretty or not. Laws are enforced in Florida for the same crime based upon your looks and of course, if you are pretty. **What the hell!!!**

The Florida courts system is so corrupt that this crime against our society can occur without so much as a whimper from the public. There was an outcry,,, but nothing major.

Had a man done this to a 14 year old girl and got no jail time the public would have burned down the courthouse. It is sad to think this can occur in modern times,,, but it has. We are all looking at the future and it is based upon your sex and how you look,,, not the crime.

Jury Tampering
To get the verdict they want

October 18, 2013

▮▮▮▮▮▮▮▮▮▮▮▮▮▮▮▮▮▮▮

7530 Little Road
New Port Richey, Fl. 33654

Regarding: **Jury duty** and **your** request for suggestions to help make **your** system better.

Dear Judge ▮▮▮▮▮▮▮▮,

*On September 23, 2013, I had the privilege of being called to serve on jury duty here in Pasco County. What a learning experience that was! To begin with, if this letter sounds like it is written by someone without a high school education that would be because it is. Approximately 30 of us were called into one court room for **your jury selection**, to pick 6 jurists. While in court,* the judge explained that the court must summon 500 people to get 30. She went on to say most don't even respond and she asked all of us, if we had suggestions to help, please make them. Now please don't think I am naive and believe for one minute that you will read this letter or respond to it. I am sure her comments were rhetorical.

The process was done in two parts, calling in approximately 15 prospective jurists at a time. It was only out in the hallway after we (the first 15) were recovering from the inquisition, that I started talking to the other first 15 potential jurists and realized I was not alone in my thinking. Several of us talked about what a **sham** we had just experienced and it is regarding this point that I would like to offer my first suggestion. **1.) Change the term from jury <u>selection</u> to jury <u>rejection</u> or jury tampering.** It was clear the attorneys doing the **rejection** were doing so to find people they could manipulate. They were not looking for people with knowledge or experience but people with brains of putty and mush. These attorneys were setting the stage for their case with jurists who they could control.

Attorneys seem to love to tell stories, so let me offer you some **foundation** for my first suggestion. Sometime in the late eighties I loved to go to a certain restaurant in Tampa that served good food and at a good price. One day I ordered a steak like I had before and they brought me a steak knife that would not cut butter. I asked for a better knife and I was told they could not bring me a sharp knife because they had been **sued** for that and lost the case. Seems someone cut them themselves with a steak knife and the restaurant lost the case. I asked, "<u>Who does not know</u> a knife is sharp and can cut you?" He shrugged his shoulders. I then said, "You do know I won't come back here if I have to bring *my own utensils." Six months later this chain of about thirty restaurants went out of business; A loss of close to one thousand jobs. How could this happen I wondered, who does not know a knife is sharp?* **Jury tampering.**

More recently a fast food restaurant was sued because they served coffee hot. At the time I loved hot coffee, but it seems someone bought a cup of their hot coffee, in a Styrofoam cup and placed it between their legs while driving a car and squeezed, <u>spilling the hot coffee all over themselves</u>. The restaurant lost the case. Now, none of us can have hot coffee to go. The best we can get is cold coffee to go. I wondered where they found twelve people that don't know coffee is hot. But worse than that, <u>where did they find a judge that did not throw this case out of their court</u> on grounds of stupidity? How do you find thirteen people that stupid? **Jury tampering.**

Then there is OJ. The overwhelming evidence was twisted under the watchful eyes of a judge and effective **jury tampering**. *Many believe to this day, this man walked around among the free after he brutally cut up two people to the dismay of all of us. What has happened to the justice system in this country?* **Jury tampering**.

If each Monday I stood out front of this courthouse (your court) and passed out flyers on how to be picked as a jurist or how not to be picked, you would have me arrested for **tampering** *with* **your** *jury pool. But how is that different than what we witnessed in* **your** *courts? They systematically scratched off the potential jurist that they could not control. At the end, the first attorney asked, "Are there any questions I did not ask, that I should have?" I almost said, "Yes, you did not say what questions I should have asked that would make you rule in my favor and let me win a big settlement and get a* big payday. This all happened under the watchful eye of **your** court, which said nothing. **<u>Jury tampering</u>**.

My next suggestion has to do with summoning five hundred people to come at the same time, 7:40am and stand in line outside the courthouse until after 8:00am. What if it were raining? We were just standing there waiting and for what? Does the courthouse not open until 8:00am? So, suggestion #**2.) Open the doors <u>before</u> the time you want people to show up.** It's just common courtesy. Acknowledging that would only be true if in **your** eyes we were people, but of course we are not. We are not people with lives, jobs or feelings and not even as low as just numbers within the masses. But something worse, we are an inexcusable source of inconvenience like the Goyims - less than cattle.

We were first led back to a room that would hold, at best, fifty people and there were seventy-five of us. We were all packed into a room where we had to listen to people telling us the same thing over and over. This brainwashing session lasted for what felt like two hours. The whole time I was standing in a hot room. Suggestion #**3.) If you are planning to put seventy people in a room it should hold seventy people.** Once more it's just common courtesy, we are people not Goyims.

In your summons you could have put more information like, "We don't feed you and you can bring food and water into court." Suggestion #**4.) Add to your summons, "Bring your own lunch, bring your own water and bring coins if you want food from our snack machine."** I had no food and no water and no coins. But it's ok; I have learned to accept my role as a Goy when it comes to this government.

Then there is the money. If I try to think outside of my box, that place where all we Goyim are to live, I am resentful that **you,** the court, think $15.00 dollars a day is *fair pay. We have lives and jobs and no one makes $15.00 for a day's work. That is pre depression money, but understandable when you consider it is the government doing the doling out. I am surprised you don't make us pay for the privilege of serving jury duty.* **Oh wait, you do.** *Here we are one essential part of* **your court***,* **your** *justice system and you can't even pay us a fair amount to cover the cost of gasoline to get there. Just in case you have been living in* **your** *bubble too long now, no one makes $15.00 per day anymore. However, the federal government thinks a family of four can live on $23,350.00 per year. Only they don't tell you where. I have figured it out, you must live in a cardboard box in the woods or in your car, all four of you-in America. Yet the attorneys who are playing with what is left of this democracy make no less than $250.00 per hour or $520,000.00 billable hours per year. The judges sit there being reportedly paid $350,000.00 per year and yet a jurist, a critical part of* **your** *court makes $01.875 per hour.*

Suggestion #5.) **Pay us what you are making. $350,000.00 would work out to be $961.53 per day.** *If that were the pay of this critical part of* **your** *system, everyone summoned would show up to get their big fat unreasonable pay check... like you. (Its unreasonable, because no one is worth $1,000.00 per day.) Problem solved, no more need to summon 500 people when you only need 30. If you summoned 30 people, more likely you would get 50. But you have to come out of the dark ages when it comes to proper reimbursement. I don't remember reading in the constitution that jurist were to* **pay** *for this right while others get fat and rich serving* **their** *injustices on the rest of us. But it is understandable when one thinks of the money you are paid. Why would* **you** *want to upset the apple cart when you are eating so* *well? After all, who said justice was fair, well it's fair to you.*

*If you have not thrown this letter into the trash by now or speed-read through it and written me off as a loser wacko, suffering from disgruntled grumpy old man's disease, dementia or Alzheimer's disease, you may have realized **your** system is broken and most of **us** realized it long ago. (One more reason people don't show up for **your** summons) For **you** it is not broken and if I were being paid the big money **you** are, I would think just like **you**, "It is all just fine. Why don't the underlings think so too? After all, I am rich. If they are poor, it is their fault." But it's not fine and the problem is **you**. You permit this to go on in **your** court and you do nothing. So justice is for the rich, not the poor. How many millionaires do you know of on death row? Maybe you will think about some of the things I have said as you rattle around in the empty shell of democracy and justice offering **your** words of wisdom as **you all** pretend everything is just fine. After all, as I understand it; judges don't have to serve on jury duty, because they're rich and above the law. Judges intentional repetition in this country is above the rest of us and **above the constitution.***

If we look into the future, as this remaining shell of democracy is consumed by religion or as others refer to them as religious terrorist organizations, it is bleak to say the least. Some also believe, the largest and best at taking over governments, is the Christian church. It appears to be all about the money, power and control for them. This terrorist religion has, from the crusades to the taking over of the English and Spanish governments, all the way to the destruction of our separation of church and state. Spain enslaved thousands to work in the mines of South America to retrieve gold and silver. They killed those that would not convert to their god. To this day, when their bounty from shipwrecks are found, it is called Spanish silver or Spanish gold, not what it really is: stolen property. England on the other hand, as I understand it, was the first international drug dealer, selling Indian opium to the Chinese, for their white gold.

*They enslaved blacks and shipped them all over the world for the money. To this day, they control islands where it is legal to hide wealth from the tax man, as scam corporations or numbered accounts; all under the watchful eye of their god. When religious leaders in their church are caught having sex with little boys, reportedly, this religion covers it up and transfers these pedophiles to other churches and unsuspecting communities. Some are hidden from the law in convents and monasteries, away from **your** laws. Reportedly, per the church, the value of raping a child for years is one million dollars. They are now working from state to state forcing their laws on the rest of us. Abortion is their hot button today and they have created a hit list to murder abortion doctors, burn clinics and now have bought legislators to make it so unreasonably difficult on these abortion clinics, that they must shut down. One day, if not stopped and they are permitted to continue their aggression, you will see crosses erected in front of your courthouse to nail the unbelievers to, or my favorite, stakes, to impale people. Don't be surprised if __Sharia law__ is eventually imposed, where they will want to hold public stoning, perhaps on **your** very courthouse steps.*

You may in fact believe that my writing the beliefs of others that imply the Christian religion is a terrorist organization is appalling and there should be a law to stop them from freely speaking out. We already have so many words we can't say today in this country and in Canada this letter could be classified as spreading hatred and against their laws. It's frightening where we are all going. I am glad I am old and I will not see what you and your kids will.

While I can still speak out and before I am hauled away to **your** secret court and secret prison, I believe you and **your** court are in violation of laws governing this country. Unlike the legislators who write their own laws for **themselves**, you are still governed with the rest of us. The clearest laws you are breaking start with the labor law. The state and federal governments have set standards for compensation for labor. We were summoned to come to **your** court without compensation for the true costs, and **your** reimbursement for time worked is $01.875 per hour. Minimum wages for the 50's, perhaps, but this is 2013 and the minimum wage in this state is $7.79/hr. **Per the DEO, the minimum wage applies to all employees in the state who are covered by the federal minimum wage.** I worked 4 hours and that means your court owes me $31.16, not $15.00 plus mileage of $1.60 totaling $32.76. I am sure you have no intention of doing the right thing here and therefore I will have to go to the labor board and seek proper compensation. If I need to hire an attorney, I will seek a class action case plus punitive damages. You should know I don't make minimum wage, I am worth more than that, as are you. So fair compensation would be what you make, $1,000.00 per day. That's every day. If you should contend that I was not an employee, than you should not offer me compensation, but you did. That makes me an employee, not a slave or an indentured servant.

The next violation you committed in your court is discrimination. You discriminated against people of color, people of age and people of race. But more important, you committed the wholesale discrimination *against intelligence. Your selections do not represent a fair cross-section of people from all walks of life, but a system of rejection to alter the outcome of each trial via* **your _jury tampering_**. *Federal laws prohibiting job discrimination include, but are not limited to:*

Title VII of the civil rights act of 1964, which prohibits employment discrimination

The equal pay act of 1963 (EPA)

Age discrimination in employment act of 1967 (ADEA)

I should point out to you, your own summon states, as I remember, "You are exempt from jury duty if you are over the age of 70."

*All of this is no more than abuse of power. Someone may just hold you accountable and the thing that will come from that is you would have to obey the laws like the rest of us. After all you are just like the rest of us, only you work for **all of us**. You have taken an oath of office to enforce the laws of the land, not exempt yourself, looking the other way, when you know it is wrong. This **jury rejection system** of yours is not right and you know it. It should be replaced with a simpler system; selection of the first six or first twelve people. No interview, no names, no past exploring, just the first in the line, serve. No one should be deemed "unfit".*

As I said before, you are the problem. You, who sit in judgment of the rest of us and slowly dismantle democracy _practicing_ your trade. I have the right to speak freely.

Congress shall make no law respecting an establishment of religion or prohibiting the free exercise thereof; _or abridging the freedom of speech,_ or the press; or the right of people peaceably to assemble, and to petition the government for the _redress_ of grievances.

They have and it started within ten years of this amendment that John Adams, and others, successfully passed an act specifically written to restrict **our** free speech. It has not stopped there as each state now imposes their restrictions on the rest of us. You who judge, must stand in front of such ignorance before we are all in prison or labor camps and the book burnings start once more. I fear you are that close.

In closing, I would like you to know that as much as you like to think you are above the rest of us, you are not. That may be hard to take, but we are people, not an endless pool of things you can play with and then toss out of your sand box when you're done. You do not have this right and someone needs to tell you and stand up to you.

Even though the price of speaking up may be, the tickets that are coming. I can see every county inspector coming after me. I can see every time I drive on the street, I will get tickets. Abuse of power creates more abuse of power. Sometime I feel like I live in Russia or China. I may have lived too long. I don't like the path this country is heading down. You can see that my brain is not yet mush nor is it malleable. Therefore, I would not make a good jurist.

Govern yourself accordingly,

William J. Ryan

CC: FBI
       President of the United States
       EEOC
       Paula S. O'Neil

Medusa
Daughter of Phorcys and Ceto
Greek mythology portrayed her as a monster
with snakes growing out of her head

Marriage

Governments around the world push marriage upon its dumb downed people, because it grows a new nation. Without new babies a country ages and becomes defenseless. Japan is one example, China is another and the FAKE government, called the United States, has found another way to replace its military with immigrants. *"Come risk your life defending America's interest (Opium fields) and get a free pass to live in this FAKE country."*

Within the society of the satanic Jesuit Christian America, marriage is an (outdated) institution. It's a big money maker for the corporate society that endorses sex, for it makes babies and they are very expensive. It is estimated today's cost (2015) to raise a child to their 18th birthday, is at $250,000.00 dollars. **It should be noted, that is today dollars not the devalued dollars of 18 years from now.** That's each child over their lifetime from birth to the age of 18 years.

The cost of each child is but another detriment to the religious concept of marriage. Cultures across every continent are pulling away due to the costs. That is the only reason America is willing to help pay for some of the costs to feed children,,, for if they don't, America will end up with a nation of short weak stunted people like those in North Korea.

April 2, 2012

It was reported that the military government of North Korea is lowering its minimum height requirements to 4 ft. 7 in. It is also reported that close to **half** of the children in one province are stunted from malnutrition. *North Korea is a small isolated country* *that has a long history of being invaded. In 1871 the United States, sold to the Illuminati and created the Second Constitution and then declared war on this country. That war is still going on. It's the reason the people are starving to death.*

November 2013

In China, the **One Baby Law** was dropped and their government,,, society,,, now permits two babies. The females in that country are not having babies until later in life,,, 30s plus,,, if at all. The men don't want the expense and prefer to spend their income upon themselves. Who can blame them? The old society of marriage is crumbling. Both sides (male and female) are moving away from this social model. The Chinese government is disappointed, they had hoped of creating more money from (its people) the babies and a stronger young (military) country. *They wanted a baby boom like America had after WWII.*

Like Japan, and the United States, men and women are not having babies and the population is aging with no young to take their place. The United States devised a clever way to replace its aging population. That is to simply open the floodgates to any and all young foreigners. That is the reason we have **no immigration laws** in this country and **Sanctuary Cities**,,, to welcome cheap labor,,, increase the tax base and offer a career in the military; a whole new society of dumb-ed down dysfunction as cultures collide.

Sanctuary City; *is a concept that dates back thousands of years. It is associated with Christianity, Islam, Judaism, Buddhism, and Hinduism. In western civilizations, Sanctuary Cities (Cities of Refuge) can be traced back to the Old Testament.*

The decline of marriage is clear in the United States when one looks at the chart below.

Marriage Rate in the U.S. 1940-2007

Source: Statistical Abstracts of the United States; NCHS, National Vital Statistics Reports[20]

By this chart it becomes clear that in the satanic Jesuit Christian America, a catalyst for marriage would seem to be war. Modern day Christian crusades hell bent on crushing any and all societies not Christian,,, as well as for war profiteering,,, clearly bring men and women together.

*The recent ongoing concept of **The Great Game** has now lasted close to 200 years. It continues to pull young men and young women into it, for the greater good of these secretive Empires,,, these very old dynasties,,, only the young warriors and the innocent pay the price.*

Before World War II (per this report) 1940 little over 12 out of 1000 people were married and as the war progressed 1942 it grew to just over 13. As all able men were sent off to war, it dropped to 11 in 1944. But after the war was over in 1945, it shot up to almost 16.5. I guess both men and women were just glad to see each other and from that joy came the **Baby Boom**.

Although, marriage from that war did not last; in 1948 marriage plummeted to about 10.5, well below the pre-war numbers. Basically, those numbers dropped until 1954, when it hit 8.4. Then it slowly started to grow until that peak in 1972. This would coincide with the United States governments reported date of the Vietnam War from 1955 to 1975.

Only the truth is this, Jesuit Christian government lies to its people and the true date of the Vietnam War was in 1946,,, just after WWII. It seems that the society of Christians, Warmongers and War Profiteers ($$$$$) must have their blood in **The Great Game**.

The society behind the government (the **Deceivers**) of America must have their wars. As this war was winding down, President Nixon had set in place (1971) the war on drugs,,, to wit, there will be no end. To insure that,,, the CIA (run by the Vatican) helped deliver cocaine to the American people. As they once delivered LSD (project MK Ultra) in the 70s, they are delivering opium today.

Then there are all the covert wars that are all around the world where America sets up puppet government leaders they can control,,, for **American Interests** (oil, gas, $$$ and now opium). *The opium fields are guarded by American soldiers and opium addiction more than doubles in the world.*

As incomes failed to keep up with the falling dollar, the cost of marriage and raising children, caused men and women to pull away from matrimonial bliss, so the numbers keep dropping. As of 2007, the number is at 7.3. Soon after this came the financial crash,,, these were the last numbers that I was able to find.

The tables have been turned to such a degree that young men of today are now just pulling out of the marriage game all together. This is a disturbing trend as we move forward in time. For me, it shows just how **Socialosity** is metamorphosing into the next stage and its true self.

We are born alone, we die alone and now we will live alone as the satanic ones want it. *A life without love makes it easier to control those people.* The differences between each of us based upon our race, gender, religion, or origin on this planet and our life experiences have become full bloom within **Socialosity**.

Isolation, via religion, race, and now Gender neutral propaganda being forced upon the children is but one more attempt to create a lifetime of messed up people, therefore easer to control.

Chapter Five

Erectile Dysfunction in Young Men

The end result of a mother's love for her female child is to give her the tools to better herself and have a better life than the mother. One where her child will not make the same mistakes she did and marry poor,,, or worse,,, foolishly marry for love.

Imagine the words being said to this impressionable child's mind as she is putting on a new face from a child's makeup starter kit. *"You are beautiful,,, now you can marry a doctor or an attorney and be rich."* The child is forever lost in media promotions and her mother's dreams and goals,,, as the mother tries to live out her own fantasy through her child. Dysfunction abounds and is passed on as part of the life cycle of **Socialosity,,, Vanity**.

The **Socialosity** insanity of this lifelong man made mental disorder,,, Vanity,,, can and will start at a very early age for these young girls. Now there is not only mom on one side of an innocent child, but the **Deceivers** on the other side, pushing the dream. The Deceivers are money takers that push their (sometimes dangerous) products upon the young impressionable minds of female children. Cartoons on the national babysitter,,, television,,, push facial products at these children before they can speak, let alone understand the words being repeatedly pushed at their impressionable minds.

December 24, 2017

A new national report released this day told of a *"Kids' makeup pulled from the shelves"* of a major department store, because it was *"laced with*

Tremolite Asbestos!"

**This is a known cancer-causing substance.
Anything for a buck! There is no regulatory agency testing these products and there will most likely never be!
Why you ask,,, because that would take funds away from the Deceivers.**

These young minds are pushed deeply into **Vanity Number Two** and **Vanity Number Three,** before they have their training wheels removed from their bicycles, if they are lucky enough to own one. The manufactures of a product such as **narcissistic child cancer face paint sets,** can be bought for all ages of very young children. The brain washing becomes epidemic when it is relentlessly pushed upon them from all sides.

These young girls get it from mom, from TV, from the internet and from peer pressure,,, *"Don't you want to marry a rich doctor or attorney?"* They now skip right over, *"He is cute!"* *"I am falling in love."* *"I have a crush on him."* to *"Mom said that he will never amount to anything and I should aim higher."*

This action is one of the roots of **Socialosity** that divide men and women, pushing them even further apart than our obvious differences. It becomes so ingrained in women that they don't even try to hide their **Gold digging claws** of greed for money.

True Story; I am sitting in one of my favorite watering holes when a woman came up to me and started asking me questions. **"Where do you work? What kind of car do you drive? Are you paying any alimony?"** *(I am not making this up)* And on and on it went until I turned to her and I said, **"If you have a credit application, I would be glad to fill one out for you!"** Her response was, **"Oh I am just trying to get to know you."** And I responded, **"No you are not,,, you are trying to see if I have any money and am worth your time."** After I said that she walked away,,, Thank god!

The end result of a society that is moving from the dark ages of no global communication into the mass media. Globally connected to the world of the now and future is,,, **disconnection**,,, between a species of beings (male and female) on this planet. What was that I just said?

Unknowingly, mothers pass on their frustrations,,, disappointments,,, their 'wasted youths', (i.e. dysfunction) upon these young impressionable girls, with their newly acquired makeup Gold Digging kits. Then the child stops playing games with the neighbor boy, because he is below the mother's standards. In doing so, the mother's goal to help better her child's life has built an unobtainable goal; which becomes a wall that cannot be scaled by any male. This is the position where the complete **disconnection** occurs and the damage done is irreversible.

Look closely into the eyes of these children and you will see the foundation of anger from their disappointment, their frustration over the quest to <u>get the cash</u>,,, starts here.

These young girls cluster together at the bus stop, looking down their catty cancer kit produced noses at all the young unacceptable boys saying, **"Yeah he is cute, but he has dirty fingernails and wants to be a truck driver like his dad. I am going to hold out for a doctor like my mother said I should. I am too pretty to settle."** They don't,,, and there is where a lifetime of disappointments begin. They cannot obtain and fulfill these goals given to them by mom, peer pressure or by the media, selling **Asbestos-laced Gold digging makeup kits** to innocent children.

We see this all the time on the news,,, a sick child needs financial help and if she/he is pretty,,, help is on the way. But if the child is not pretty,,, no help,,, no air time. It would seem that ugly will not help with ratings and sell soap flakes and potato chips.

The young girls push away the boys and the boys push back. The boys learn to avoid the manufactured **clown face** beauty,,, avoid the ones with all the makeup and the detailed questions as to their fathers income and their income potential. They are quickly labeled by the girls, Catty and **Gold Diggers**, and the boys push back hard. The wall between beauty and the beast within all boys grows greater as boys learn which ones to steer clear of (by the amount of goo in their faces) referring to them as **"High maintenance"** as their division numbers grow.

If you are one of the chosen ones,,, a doctors son,,, it becomes a feeding frenzy as they take many a virgins to the sacrificial alter and nail them,,, then dump them the next day. For those boys (the rich), it becomes a game to treat the endless streams of girls like whores and the **Catty Gold Diggers** they have become,,, thanks to mom,,, friends, as well as the media.

As unacceptable boys are pushed away and then build walls to push back, the remarks get ugly. Dad tells some boy what he thinks of these girls, passing on his frustrations dealing with rejections (based on income) in the past. The war between the beauty and the beast leaves the boys to play together as they start to enter manhood.

Video games of racing cars,,, war, killing cops and Muslims, become the paramount educators of their young life as they discover porn and themselves. These unobtainable females on both sides; reality and imagination, help to enforce the concept of the ideal female for them.

Now both sides are not able to find their imaginary life partner,,, their soul mate,,, and many just give up. Therein lies the bazaar result of **Vanity Number Three,** creating unforeseen damage,,, **Erectile Dysfunction** in young boys. Pay close attention to this,,, for this is the first glimpse into our state of the art, electronic, **Socialosity** planets population or the end of breeding with each other.

Some reports indicate male dysfunction is a growing disorder not seen at these **new levels** before. They blame it on video games, porn and of course the drug industry. I also put the blame on the dysfunction of mom and dad, peer pressure and the **Deceivers** that will take money, manufacturing products for young females with impressionable minds, helping to set lifelong unobtainable goals on both sides.

It is estimated, by some Sexologists that the problems with young male potency have climbed to between 30 and 50 percent. This is in an age group from between fifteen years old to twenty years old.

: : : : : : : : :

One of the goals of the satanic Agenda 21 is to reduce the world population, which is being aided by GMO foods. These grains and other products will reduce the sperm count in rats and then within 3 generations the reproductive abilities, killing off the species.

: : : : : : : : : :

This male disorder is normally not seen until middle age or in the elderly. The rift between the sexes grows, as the unseen disorder of Socialosity spreads around the globe, as it has within the past few years.

Even when a young couple find each other or settle for each other, the damaged male,,, now married,,, in today's society, would prefer video games over sex with his partner. Per one report, it is estimated to be **fully one third of all young males would rather play video games than have sex with their partners**. She sits at her **Vanity** table or the table of goo and he sits with his phone in hand or in front of the TV. The trained dysfunctions of **Socialosity** are now life-long.

We have moved from a dysfunctional society to a closed individual group of people. The next generation don't look at each other, don't speak to each other and the skills of verbal commutation become a lost art,,, much like *script writing has become*. If we don't teach it,,, we lose it.

The end result is Socialosity in all its levels moves ever closer to its true essence. This have now manifested itself into such a level of dysfunction that young articulate intelligent males are not breeding or producing. Only the poor,,, ones that can't afford video games and little missy vanity makeup cases, will happily find each other and reproduce.

The others will be spending a lifetime searching for the one they could never find. Sitting frustrated in front if a Vanity mirror,,, while their partner becomes lost in a world of make believe, filled with fast moving wars, battles, car chases and mechanical females.

As societies suffering from all four stages of **Socialosity**, we are moving away from each other (male/female). If somehow those in the future should survive the **Sixth Die Off** that is just years away, they will require more skills in artificial insemination. More manufactured people will become the norm as the ones that survive,,, if any,,, build the **New Master Race** from what is left of the damaged DNA. The greatest experimentation with our DNA is and has accrued as we ingest all manner of unregulated drugs, enriching the pharmaceutical industry deceivers.

NICA
National Infrastructure Advisory Council

At the end of 2018, a group of bright people are preparing all of us for the Great Black Out. Under this Black out, planned for 2019, the whole country is to become dark. No power means, no water, no food, no gasoline, meaning chaos will erupt on the land.

The FEMA Death Camps will open up and move into high gear killing the masses,,, the Eaters as they call them. For the first time, these children from this generation will find themselves powerless. The dysfunction will force them to look over at their partners and they will have to talk to each other.

A power outage will be much like the Project MK Ultra of the late 50s, wherein the Jesuit Vatican controlled CIA wanted total control over their property,,, us,,, and began to distribute this drug to the young masses. The goal was mind control and the end result was the opposite,,, rebellion.

In a total power outage,,, it would force the strong ones together and they would fight back. The weak one,,, the Eaters,,, will march into the FEMA Death camps.

Chapter Six

Gay

We all are people trying to live in a real dysfunctional satanic mess we inherited.

We have been brainwashed by religion designed to provide us with distractions, so we don't see what is truly going on in the world. It is time to open your eyes so you may see,,, the truth.

We as members of many multiple societies (boxes) attempt to blend with others unlike us, then we freely move (under camouflage) from one society to the other. Sometimes without noticing, we discover many types of humans living in harmony, in spite of the differences.

The lies told to us by the narcissistic (some satanic) religious leaders *(evil always raises to the top)* within all cults wanting to control us, (power and money) are uncovered and history is rewritten once again, exacerbating the lies. As our world becomes more of a metropolis, we all become more tolerant of each other with new knowledge, more open-minded and understanding.

The old social ways of the bible thumpers are to die out within one pod of beings, as more humane ways are accepted or forced upon the other unforgiving satanic hardliners. The old becomes the new as defects are discovered and the intolerant are forced to bend or break, standing firm upon their satanic roots with the willingness to throw people away.

To discard another because they do not fit into **their conceived ideals** of what the world should look like,,, *(their unforgiving gods views)* are passed on or pushed upon us all with **Laws Of Intolerance**. Unfortunately today, religious cults rule the land across the globe and all of us suffer from these nut jobs. The ones suffering the most from the destructive **Level Four** of **Scrupulosity** are willing to do or say anything to stop the other religions being forced upon the rest of the world. Hence, wars over god and all the killing in the world today.

To understand more look up the Jesuit Oath (as an example) and see the satanic words there in plain sight for all to see. This is one cult (box) overlapping another pretending to be good while taking an oath to make war and kill babies.

**Just so you understand,,,
this Oath should bother you!!!**

: : : : : : : : : :

Sodomy Law

Religion has played a devastating role in its attempts to combat homosexual activity for thousands of years. Those that stand next to god always seem to have all the answers to all the questions. Same sex activity goes against god himself,,, per these destructive uncompromising lost religious people. *Pull back and observe the hate, intolerance, evil and satanic solutions to one of god's creatures.*

Those within the cult of the Christian religious community are such hypocrites and two oxymoron examples are; 1) *A religion where it hides and protects child pedophiles.* 2) *Assisting the Nazis out of Europe* *after WWII on the **Ratlines or Rat Trails** and providing them with new names and pass ports from the **Red Cross**.*

How any thinking person can be a member of this destructive catholic cult is beyond me. How can they not see what is just before them,,, the truth? This is clearly a satanic cult,,, the Jesuits that took over the Roman Catholic church in the 16th century.

They are the epitome of evil. In fact, they know all and see all. They intend to force their satanic religion on the rest of us,,, believing their justification is,,, god's will. **(Satan is a god as well.)** The following is a quote from a Christian Pope leader, standing next to god **(?)** himself.

*"**Homosexual activity is an affront to god and those people are damned to burn in hell for their actions against god.**" And yet they do this to children within their church!!!*

Those words don't much sound like a loving and forgiving god,,, do they? Therefore, I just don't understand why a gay person would ever become a Christian, knowing this cult's views on these "***throw away***" people.

In 1075 (Christian time), a man who had intercourse with his brother in arms would be turned into a eunuch. *A eunuch is a man that has been castrated.* Sometimes this was done at an early age so that the person could perform a specific social function. Most were made guardians of women or the harem servants, to insure no sexual activity,,, spread of disease,,, or unwanted babies happened.

The Buggery (sodomy, sexual activity between a person and a non-human animal) **Act of 1533** made homosexual acts a capital offence until 1861. The last two sodomites were hanged in 1835, for their crimes against god and the Christian religion, which was being forced upon these people. *God's love has such a strange way of showing his face through the faithful within this cult,,, as well as others.*

Well into the 1950s, the police enforced laws prohibiting homosexual behavior. By 1954, there were over one thousand men in prison in England and Wales for their "**Homosexual Offences.**" Stop and think,,, that was not that long ago.

Only in 1952, when the high profile arrest and trial of **Alan Turing,** a mathematician and World War II code breaker, was convicted was there enough shame placed upon the **Christian Society** to bend the Christian laws against god,,, taking away their power over the people. Alan Turing helped save these people and their country. The next generation would find compassion, forgiveness, tolerance and understanding,,, outside of the church,,, long after his death.

In 1967, the United Kingdom Parliament repealed Buggery Laws for England and Wales. *The tight hold of the satanic Jesuits began to lose their control (just a little) over the population as kindness, understanding and enlightenment moved in to replace it. They, the satanic ones, are running in fear.*

In 2009, the Prime Minister issued an apology on behalf of the British **Christian** government for *"the appalling way he was treated."* It was long in coming and well too late for **Alan Turing,** for he had committed suicide in 1954 while under government ordered **homosexual treatment**. He was forced to take female hormones,,, a chemical castration was ordered by an intolerant and unforgiving **JESUIT** Christian run government.

I would hope by now that you have recognized the movement from a violent **Level Four** Socialosity, within this hypocritical Christian run society, to a more tolerant (yet still nuts) **Level Three**. They (the religious sheeple), under the satanic ones) are discovering that in order to survive,,, (save the Jesuit cult) they must blend with other more powerful loving and forgiving societies so as to keep the money coming in. *Can't stop the money*.

When the injustice of a religion and its intolerance for those that go against its teachings (beliefs) is recognized,,, the movement away from that religion is felt in Rome. The powers behind the Jesuit Pope begins to lose control over the masses,,, and most importantly the **money**,,, not the souls of the faithful. *That is what religion is all about,,, power,,, ability to "make and wage relentless war" and control over people and their money.*

This Jesuit Christian forced society, suffering from all four stages of **Scrupulosity**, is intolerant of homosexual activity and yet welcomes such acts, committing these very same crimes against children, within the hallowed halls of this Jesuit cult religion. Their massive cover-up of these crimes *(paying hush money to the victims)* did not silence public opinion. In 2014, the present pope was ordered by the **United Nations** to *"release the names and countries of origin"* of these child rapist priest's, so they could be prosecuted and the Pope said **no!** The Christian priest child rapists are still out there, undoubtedly raping children all over the world. The ignorance and intolerance still follow this faith,,, as their gods look on.

What must their god think of their actions to cover up these crimes against children?

Stop and think for a moment,,, if their god is the anti-Christ,,, Satan,,, Lucifer,,, or the Devil,,, the Jesuit Pope's actions to cover this all up would make more sense.

If a society is of one religion,,, Christian,,, and its government is also Christian,,, it will not enforce the laws to protect children,,, if it attracts that religion. **Separation of church and state is the FIRST amendment to the United States Constitution,,, the first!!!**

There is not a better place to go if you are a child rapist, than the Jesuit run Christian church. They welcome pedophiles with open arms and will criminally defy all, protecting their cult society. This act is **Level Four of Socialosity** as well as **Level Four of Scrupulosity**. The cults of all religions have parallels found within all societies. They cross between, moving freely and unnoticed by most, caught up in these religious cults. Most only see heaven,,, the religion,,, not the ailment, the illness, the sickness within this disease and disorder of scrupulosity.

Other very old societies, well over 10,000 years old, have found other ways to accept all within the tribe of man. These people that were not exterminated by the Christian' as savages,,, welcomed all. What a foreign and bazaar concept to all modern religions,,, **all** to be welcomed.

Native American Tribes
Or
Indigenous People of the
New Land

Pre-Columbian Era: Whenever I write of these people it is always with great respect and I never use western terms, names or labels if I can avoid them. These are the only humans that can truly lay claim to this **"New Land,"** for they walked here first over 40,000 years ago. These indigenous people and their cultures were exterminated, diminished or extensively altered by Europeans and their **Christian gods**. Their quest was to

kill the savages in order to steal their gold, silver and land.

Indigenous People of the New Land should be more respected.

Some societies that have been around for thousands of years are not trying to take over the world and killing all those that stand in their way; I would add their satanic gods way,,, have adopted different, more respectful, tolerant principles for their people,,, all people. Most all of these **Indigenous** tribes understood and blended with nature. They tried to live peacefully next to each other since, before the Christians, before Romans, before Judaism and before the Pyramids were built.

Within some of these exterminated indigenous tribes, there are **four types of people** and all were welcomed into the tribe.

1. The **Warrior Male** would hunt and provide food for all the tribe.
2. The **Cook and Child Care Female** would stay at the camp.
3. The **Warrior Female** would hunt and provide food for the tribe.
4. The **Cook and Child Care Male** would stay at the camp.

All of these types (male, female, gay, cross dressers) were welcomed and **not judged**, for they all provided something to the **whole** of the tribe, **unlike all the modern, religious, narcissistic societies of today.** One Native American Tribe leader said, ***"Only the white man has throw away people."*** *Those words should cut you like a knife unless your soul is that twisted and damaged from the god people.*

Today, as we sit back and review history with 20/20 hindsight, it is clear why these people were slaughtered, their lands stolen and their cultures (societies) erased from the face of the Earth and they were labeled savages. When the good Christians came to the **"New Land"**, they offered the **"Savages"** (as they were called) the opportunity to become Christian or have their arm cut off. One day, it was recorded that over 400 refused, paying for that decision with their lives. Modern day history books,,, written by Christians,,, will omit those bits of factual information that damage the society of their satanic religion. To this day, they are still rewriting history. I would add, so much so that there is not enough time to get their new spin straight between them, (keeping all the lies straight).

"Become a Christian or we will cut off your arms!"

Why anyone would embrace this brutal enslaving Jesuit Christian religion defies every fiber of my logical being. Do people really need an old man in the sky to save them that bad? Try to remember they protect pedophiles,,, they helped move thousands of Nazis out of Europe on the Rat Trail, because the Nazis are Christians. They gave them **absolution**,,, a new name and a legal passport from the Red Cross so they could avoid prosecution.

Enlightenment

As communication improves around the globe, each one of us is discovering the many lies told to us by all of our religious run governments and the Deceivers within. Their fear of the masses is so great that in America during the 1960s, the **CIA** tried to control its people with **LSD** under code name **Project MK Ultra, a mind control program**. Do you really think they have ever stopped? At this present day, the Jesuit Christian run headless beast government provides them with a blank check each year.

Making each one of us fit into a box that they can control is still going on to this very day. The only purpose I can conceive of is once more,,, money and power over all or part of **The Great Game**.

The money, time and effort spent trying to cure Gays from being Gay is horrific at best. All one has to do is apply logic and reasoning to how the human is created,,, and please let's leave out the gods. Just take god and religion out of your thinking and look at the process of making a replicate of yourself.

Yin and Yang Energy

The Chinese philosophy, Yin and Yang Energy, dark-light, negative-positive, male-female,,, dates back thousands of years; only helps to support the logic needed to understand how we are what we are. For this you must think outside of the box they (the **Deceivers**) have built for you and others to live within and the limited knowledge they provide you for understanding.

It has been recorded that sometimes the soul enters the body with male energy, sometimes with female energy and sometimes a perfect balance of each. However, one must remember the human body is a mixture of chromosomes from each totally different type of beings,,, male and female.

These chromosomes create us and help determine the physical sex of the body,,, not the soul within the body. This balance is not always perfect and will create ranges that the soul must adapt to. We are much more than our temporary physical bodies that have been made for the spirit that is in each of us.

Some women look and act like men,,, some men look and act like a women. That is not bad or wrong, or something "that must be cured." It should be accepted like the Indigenous Tribes (those "savages") once did before the good Jesuit Christians killed them all and their gods.

I have created a Chromosome Chart to represent the full spectrum of possibilities of the human body. The physical body, made for the soul, can and will fall within this range and sometimes a mixture may occur. This is perfectly normal and will require you to use a healthy, open and intelligent mind to see, understand and accept this knowledge.

Please leave your bigoted, racist, religious, hatred and bias behind, for just a moment and pretend you are coming to this idea with a fresh, clean and open mind,,, like that of a child,,, if you can still do such things.

Chromosome Chart

There are three aspects; the physical body, the sexual self-awareness (sometimes brought with us in this life) and the soul. All of us as we enter this life fall some place between the male and female spectrum, as the spirit brings its own history to this temporary life.

The problem is,,, the Deceiver,,, the ones wanting total control over you,,, dictate right and wrong and mix with it a lot of hate and heartlessness. With a snap of their fingers, the masses are ready to kill all left handed babies and those that don't fit into their bodies "as god designed them."

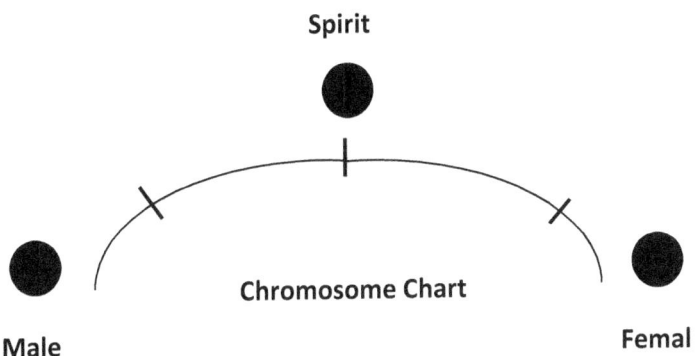

Spirit

Chromosome Chart

Male

Femal

Human DNA Strand

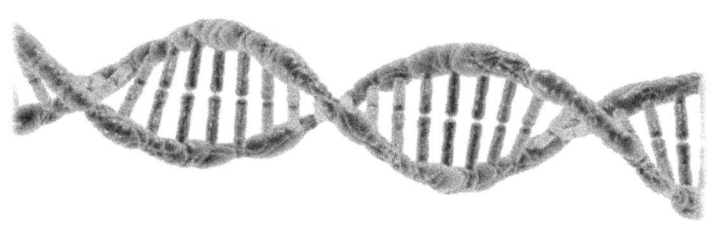

The physical brain falls within any part of this range and confusion may occur as the spirit,,, the soul, tries to fit within the newly acquired body and sometimes they clash. The soul, the spirit of each of us may bring its own energy, overriding the brains wiring to the physical body.

True story: One man was born with two 'Y' chromosomes and as an adult male, married to a woman, working as a linesman, transformed into a woman within a few short years. He had no control over this and accepted the change from man to woman,,, growing breasts on his own,,, then having a sex change.

Transgender people have a gender identity or gender impression that is different from their physical body's sex. The mind is saying one thing and the body is saying another. The soul or spirit may say something different as well and is trying to adjust within the physical brain and physical body.

Today, as we enter the more **Enlightened Time**, a more understanding time, we all become more excepting of others and their souls, (regardless of religion or government) their spirit struggles to feel right within their physical body and mind, that they inherited. This requires them to push back against that society's religion, its hatreds and biases.

It must be clear to you by now that **all** major religions suffer from some level of **Scrupulosity**. Applying those same **four levels** upon societies across the globe, the madness of daily events unfolding before our eyes, become clearer.

We can understand when we see the bigger picture and apply these same principals of madness within all religions to the madness within all social clicks, groups, clubs, races, unions, corporations, politics and governments. We are all suffering from **Socialosity**,,, (including me) in our own way,,, (on a singular level) and don't see it, for we are living it. You must pull back and observe your actions and determine if they are yours or old recordings passed on to you from the Deceivers.

In the upcoming **6th Die Off**,,, that is but a few short years away,,, adjustments must be made or extermination of **all** species of life will become the outcome (as is unfolding before our eyes today). Either we accept each other in peace and try to undo the damage done by the **Deceivers** or we die under the unseen destructive power of **Socialosity**.

Chapter Seven

Review

Socialosity

$\mathbf{R}$egardless of all the many different dysfunctional societies on Earth that we are born into,,, country, religion, race or color (to name but a few), each has four levels within each of them. It would seem each of us is so different, yet so much the same. In fact, many times it is found that we are not clean, empty vessels (as some believe) to be filled,,, with clean empty souls or spirits.

Those in the physical that have come many times before us, the old souls, know there is much more to life than we can see,,, and therefore requires each one of us to look with open minds, leaving behind our inherited prejudices from all the global societies.

There is much more going on to this thing we call life than meets the eye. So, in order to see, one must look,,, for most of us raised among the bigotries and lies of our forefathers, in order to justify their atrocious actions, (of that society over another) we have closed our minds to the truth that deep in our souls, we already know. Even though it is staring us in the face,,, right before our eyes.

Therein lay the first need into opening all the closed doors. Otherwise, these closed doors will remain closed by the ones unwilling to give up the comfort of what they were given by their society and firmly believe in or want to save their position ($$$). Giving up that foundation is why change comes very often, hard, to late and at to high of a price,,, if at all.

The intensity of **re**writing history by one society over another (by the **Deceivers** within) is clear when we look at one of the most destructive and destabilizing religions on the planet The Christian's or more so, the Roman Catholic religion and its crusades,,, was taken over by the satanic Jesuits, as this Christian cult encompasses all religions.

They would have us believe that their last crusade ended in the 15th century, when in fact,,, in these present days we are still living among the lies passed down from one dysfunctional societal generation to the next dysfunctional, murdering, war profiteering society generation.

History is being re-written once more, for we are present day in a Christian crusade, killing Muslims. The pretense of the end of the crusades just happens to coincide with the arrival of the satanic Jesuits,,, "make and wage relentless war."

Each new society generation believers in the lies passed down,,, press on with the goal of killing all those that stand in the way, (non-believers) apposing their inherited societal religions,,, forced upon them at birth. *They have no choice but to believe, for they have been brainwashed from birth and all through childhood.*

The **Indigenous People of the New Land,** were called savages, when in fact they have a better understanding of life and its cycles than we do today. Remember, they lived in harmony with all their people and all other life.

We, who were raised within the western, intently defective, societies,,, brainwashed from birth with lies,,, struggle with **Socialosity** all of our adult lives. We may never get past the walls erected by our forefathers, passed on as *"the way things are and you should not fight them or you will become an outcast."*

Socialosity is the understanding of all four stages of growth within all inherently defective societies. Regardless of our nation, race, religion, color, creed or even species of life; birds of a feather flock together. We are attracted to like beings, like spirits and therein lay the societies needed rights over each other.

If you happen to be a pelican, a rat, an ant or a wolf, you most likely run in some form of a pack. This offers protection from the ones unlike those in the pack and life gets better, for each takes care of the other via these needed rights (laws, rules). There is truly safety in numbers,,, (numbers being of the same species) from the one un-like you,,, that want to kill you and your kind.

Within each society, size does matter for the most part, but when respect of the others is lost, leadership can change. One such example that comes to mind is the Kangaroo society, where the biggest male rules and breeds within his harem of females. He battles younger males for leadership of this one particular mob (groups of kangaroos are called mobs). When in this case a young smaller male tried to take over, he was quickly put down by this big ruling male.

When the battle was over he returned for some consoling and sex with his females and was rejected by them all. The rules of that society changed by the masses and they ousted the big male without a fight. The leader was overthrown by rejection.

He left the mob and all that he knew his whole life behind him. The Jill's (female roos) are left to the mercy of the pack of young inexperienced males and dispersed. Rejected, the big buck or boomer, left the society that he had spent most of his entire life with, to find another society that would accept him,,, people.

He moved into a residential subdivision, eating garbage and when people saw the big scarred up old male,,, they began to feed him. So, this became his new life,,, his retirement in a new society that would have him.

The people knew he was a big older male with many scars of many battles, but must have lost the last one. When in fact, he won that battle but he had lost their (Jill's) respect. He lived for a short time in the wilds of that subdivision,,, that society that would have him, until he was hit by a car and killed; finally, freed from being an outcast.

He was already dead when the females rejected him (his society, all that he knew, kicked him out) for whatever reason. Proving size does not matter. Even a total corrupt religion like the Christians, can be exposed for what they are and those lost souls can be brought to the light of intelligence with perseverance kicking and screaming and still not see the light.

December 20, 2017

It was reported on this day that Cardinal Archbishop **Law** passed to his **Just Deserves** and now must face God himself for the cover up of child abuse by priests. He is responsible for moving pedophile priests, caught raping children, from one parish to another parish. What do you think God is saying to him right now?

1. Good job,,, you protected the good name of the church and all of its money.
2. You sickening bastard,,, burn in hell for the pain you inflicted upon the innocent children that trusted you to do the right thing,,, protect them!!!

My guess is it would depend upon your society, if you are a Christian or not, as to how you would answer that question, interpreting this god's thoughts.

My personal thinking is there is no heaven,,, there is no hell,,, there is only life experience and the acquired memories we accumulate. There is no right or wrong and certainly no punishment, but that inflicted here among the living. Just in case I am wrong,,, stop and think,,, would you really want to go and spend eternity in a heaven created by the Jews so you (the Goyim) may serve and be surrounded by religious pedophiles welcomed with open arms??? I personally will pass and you can find me on the outskirts of the far reaches of the known universe as far away from people and their pathetic, hateful, ignorant lives as I can get.

In my book ***Jesus Christ in Canaan***, I detailed (in story format) the ***Deceivers*** (a society of greed and control, laced throughout all other societies around the world) within the church and governments. They push war for profit, killing its own people for this one religion. This same group of **Deceivers** re-wrote the schoolbook for the young and change the truth to meet their Christian agenda; thereby creating a whole new generation of Christian warriors to continue the crusade, blindly killing for these Gods.

As Adolf Hitler (a good Christian) **said, "He alone who owns the youth, gains the future."**

The truth is lost within each society and only when we move from one to the other, do we see and find the truth,,, according to a different society suffering from the four stages of their particular **Socialosity**. This new, more global prospective, helps us to find intersecting points of fact, unmasking the lies being taught to each of us, each and every day of our lives by the Deceivers.

In Japan after WWII, their next generation of young, were not taught of their full part in the war (like we in the United States that have been shown only a small part of the truth) and for this next generation that history was reduced (as I understand) to something like two lines in their history books. In doing so, that society, much like the American society, rewrote their history and the **Deceivers** move on to the next pile of cash,,, undetected. You see each society is suffering from **Socialosity** and for those raised within this Japanese bubble, (this rewrite of their history), are struck in the face when they travel, discovering the atrocities and shame of what their forefathers had done and they knew nothing of. Their idyllic life crashed and their belief system shattered, they return home in silence bearing much shame.

History is full of examples of society collapsing when introduced to one that looks better, (the grass is always greener on the other side of the fence). When the

Spanish invaded the New Land they call South America in 1492 (Christian time), the empires there that had ruled with an iron fist, collapsed. All of the followers changed sides, moving away from what they perceived as a ruthless regime.

Most found themselves going from the frying pan into the fire. They were enslaved by the satanic Christian that found them to be subhuman and rated them by their color (See the La Casta chart). Labeling them all as savages makes it easier for the troops, the masses following in the Christian cult faith, to kill them and take their land, their women, their gold and their silver. I would add,,, still clamming it as theirs (Spanish) to this very day. There is just no end to their shame.

Hundreds of thousands of the **Indigenous people of the New Land** were enslaved to produce silver that was taken to Spain. As I understand it, if you laid the bodies of the dead enslaved indigenes people head to toe, it would form a line that stretched from South America to Spain. The Spanish Christian's did this unapologetically. They give not a single thought to those that paid with their lives, just to retrieve that sliver.

If those acts are not satanic,,, if killing, enslavement, rape, murder and theft are the acts of a good loving god,,, what are the acts of a devil god?

Today, the Spanish government still claims the sunken ships filled to the upper deck with this ill-gotten gain of treasure as theirs. Every time I see anything made of silver, I see the blood dripping from it. I think of all those slaves that paid for it with their lives, because the society of the Spanish Christians had enslaved them. They enslave us still today, with their lies and deception.

Every race, every culture, every living creature, lives within a culture, within a society under the rules of eat or be eaten. Only the human parasitic society has its **Four Levels of Socialosity**.

Only with enlightenment can we all rise above the hatred and bigotries passed down from the ones that came before us, the **Deceivers,** in all levels of society. Each of us must find our own way through all the lies.

From an early age of 4 or 5, I learned not to trust the things that my small mob,,, my so called dysfunctional family had taught me. For it all, every sentence was full of lies. When I asked these people that I was raised by, why they lied to me, their response was always, laughter. It was some kind of a joke and I was somehow entertaining for them.

In public, when I was asked a question I would always act stupid and say, "I don't know." Not until I had heard the answer from three other people, (outside the family) would I believe I had the right answer or knowledge; and even then, not fully believing it to be true.

That is no way to raise a child, but it made me keenly untrusting and extremely good at ferreting out the truth. I taught myself to always look for patterns of lies to find the truth. Relentlessly, searching for the truth,,, the real truth behind the lies.

That mistrust carried on into adulthood and became a strand of the fabric of my life, as I search for the truth in everything,,, ferreting out the lies. The truth is very allusive; just when I believe that I have the truth in hand, I discover more lies, more half-truths. Then the war to sort it all out continues. The layers of deception never seem to have a bottom and I believe they carry on well into the afterlife. *Just when you think you know,,, there is another layer to the onion.*

It is such an uphill battle for all of us to find the allusive truth, as we move into a global society. Knowledge is, for most of us, at our fingertips and we all are left to sort out the fact from the endless fiction. The false news,,, the false history is recorded and believed by so many and even as I write these words, history is being rewritten,,, again.

What is the answer? Recognizing the Four intense Levels of **Socialosity** for one thing and taking everything with a grain of salt. For even my words and my efforts to find the truth are slanted in the fact that I don't trust any system of government, religion or judicial system. My words are biased by my past, but my efforts are true and sincere.

I,,, like so many before me, just want the truth, we want to expose the many **Deceivers** for what they are.

But they are many, very strong and powerful, they seem to own and control everything.

I would add that even when I do expose them and require them to obey the laws set down to protect us all, they ignore my words and the perpetuation of evil that always rises to the top, continues to pretend our social system is working just fine. When in fact it is broken and we all know it, but look the other way. I detailed this discovery in a book that I wrote called, **Victimize the Victim**.

Denial is another branch within all levels of **Socialosity**, for even when we know in our hearts, deep within our souls,,, we still carry out these crimes against others. Either within our society or within another society,,, wrong is wrong.

One such example of our souls not adjusting to what we have been taught (lies) is found within the American suicide rate among the military veterans. Those veterans of the most recent battles for oil, opium/poppies and money; as well as another ongoing Christian crusade killing Muslims as part of **The Great Game** that began in January of 1830. The truth is a hard pill to swallow when they return home, sworn to secrecy, unable to tell the truth of what is happening there.

After years of facing the atrocities committed by this FAKE American government in foreign lands and the utter and complete hatred of the American invaders within their countries,,, it is just too much. Think of how they must feel when we were first told of the Taliban forcing farmers to grow the poppy plants that produce opium. First, American soldiers destroyed the plant and later they were told to stand guard over the **Opium** plants, for they are now "**American Interest's**" to drug and dumb up its people. Many believe that it is done all under the watchful eyes of the CIA,,, part of the master plan.

Today, these plants are being produced to enrich the pharmaceutical industry, to the pleasure of the **CIA** that wants to find a new source to control the population. The **CIA** did this before with **LSD**, then with **Cocaine,** helping to ship it into America. Now this country stands guard over this drug **Opium**, causing whole communities within our society to collapse,,, (Socialosity **Level Four**). Perhaps that is the real reason we are in that country, **The Great Game,,,** power,,, over the people in this foreign land and now the bounty that comes with drug addiction of its own people.

Some estimates report the number of people addicted to opium has <u>doubled</u> in the past few years.

This FAKE American satanic, Jesuit, Christian run government, filled with psychotic self-enriching **Deceivers,** is an example of the full extent of **Level Four** of **Socialosity**. These lecherous sociopath-psychopathic politicians are in government to get as much money for themselves as they can carry. One was quoted as saying, *"We create laws for ourselves. We don't have to obey the laws for the public."*

This is because the District of Columba is a City-State, therefore not part of America. Like London England and the Vatican,,, all City-States,,, parasites that suck the blood out of the rest of us.

Evil always rises to the top. Seeing each stage of this disorder, I believe can only help expose the truth for all of us.

The Devils Triangle

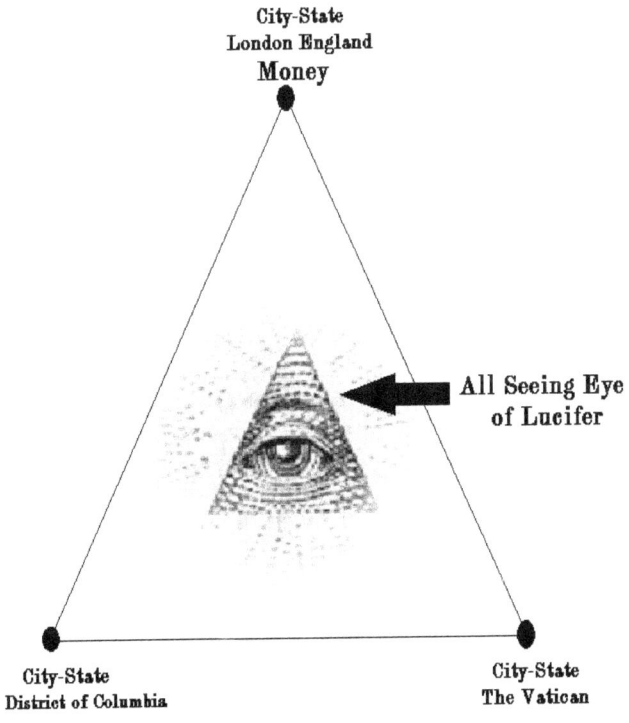

City-State
London England
Money

**All Seeing Eye
of Lucifer**

City-State
District of Columbia

City-State
The Vatican

The All Seeing Eye of
Lucifer

Ratlines

Rat-lines; were a system of moving **Nazi** war criminals from Europe to places across the globe. The **Vatican** played an enormous part in providing sanctuary to these war criminals. *This is most distressing to take in.* First the **Vatican** gave each **Nazi** war criminal,,, **ABSOLUTION**,,, (forgiveness, pardon, exoneration, clemency, mercy) from guilt and punishment in the **Christian** eyes. Then they gave them a new identity, name address and history. Finally, they passed them on to the **RED CROSS** that issued each a pass port to their freedom. Their crimes against humanity were rewarded with freedom and as much **Jewish stolen gold** as they could carry.

Someone please tell me,,, how can you walk the face of this earth and call yourself a Christian?

Check out Google images type in Christian Leaders Saluting Hitler and see what you find.

https://bishopjenky.wordpress.com/tag/priests/

Chapter Eight

The Future

The future is not hard to predict. All one must do is look into the past to see into the future. There are countless examples from brilliant writers that could see into our future and warn us of the paths we are on. The first one that comes to my mind is Herbert George Wells, born September 21, 1866 and died on August 13, 1946. What would he have seen in his lifetime?

As an English writer, he would have seen two wars that invaded his country and the untold indiscriminate killing of the innocent all around him. The one story that comes to mind is **The Time Machine,** completed and published in 1895 (before both world wars). By some reports it reflected the present times and views of past more peaceful times in his life. A life when one could think of our place on earth without the demented Deceivers crushing mankind for power and money.

The blend of his personal, socialist and political views of the future, as well as industrial pollution and the decay of the future social degeneration are mixed within his gripping story from this time. The story contained the views,,, at that time,,, of the dying earth as well as the end of the world and ultimate destiny of humankind. It was popular fiction at this time and he blended them into this story.

The **Talking Rings** told of a time when all the air would be used or destroyed, most likely by the 300 plus year war, that devastated the planet. *(Perhaps he was referring to **The Great Game** war of present day)* He must have also witnessed the war profiteering of his time and those that live just under the surface, living off of the flesh of the (***government de-education system and state sponsored religion***) ignorant, sent off to fight in the wars that enriched all of the satanic Deceivers.

In his lifetime the division of religion was strong and in a Jesuit Christian run country, there is to be but one God and it is not to be a Jew god. The **French** and the **British Mandate for Palestine** literally stole land from the Ottoman Empire, Nablus, Vilayet of Syria and gave it to the Jews, forming a Jewish National Homeland. ***They murdered the people, stole their land and gave it to the Jews to get the Jews out of their countries. Or was it to create more conflict in order to enrich their war enterprises?***

Were the Jews that powerful, running this from just under the surface? Or did the Christian despise the Jews that much (**Jewish Deicide**) and were willing to invade another weaker country to give away their land so as to get the Jews out of their Christian country?

Think for a moment,,, where did the good Jesuit Christians send the indigenes people in the new land? The ones they did not kill,,, the savages,,, they herded them like livestock,,, into pins with standing room only and pushed them out west on small plots of land. There in the blazing sun they were meant to die. There plans were successful, for most have done just that,,, died off. Their true stories of genocide,,, never to be told.

Jewish Deicide:

The belief among some Christian's was that the Jewish people, <u>as a whole,</u> were responsible for the murder of the only son of god,,, Jesus. In Germany, during the Second World War, the good Jesuit Christian's chanted "**God Killer**" as they drug the Jewish people (men, women and children, old and young alike) out into the streets and herded them into cattle cars to their deaths. The hate did not go away with the end of the war,,, it is still there in the hearts of many good God fearing Christians, just waiting for a chance to return. The ignorance, biases and hatred are passed on to each of the children and the cycle continues.

I do not understand how 2.5 billion people can be filled with so much hate. Today, that hate is turned towards the Islamic people. They seem to love war and killing,,, so glad to send their children off to war for American interest,,, you know,,, like opium.

This would have been the talk of the time (**The Great Game**). Perhaps they set the ground work for the endless war within the story. *I would add the same one we are fighting to this very day,,, over 100 years later. Another genocide in the name of the Roman Catholic (Jesuit) Church,,, killing for god and enriching the satanic 1%ers.*

When I look at this story (The Time Machine) the Morlocks that live underground feeding off of the Eloi, the childlike vegetarian people; am I seeing Mr. Wells' interpretation of the **Deceivers, (of that time)** the ones that pull the strings behind every government? **Deceivers**: The ones (religion, insurance, pharmaceutical and war industries) hidden behind the scene, just out of sight, directing the ignorant, safe from view, sucking the life out of the de-educated ignorant for yet more wealth.

Are the meat-eating, underground, cave dweller Morlocks, another reflection of the times he lived in? Are they the Jews, forced to live in exile by the good Jesuit Christians, feeding upon the flesh of the Goyim? What was in his mind?

What could he have seen that guided him to create such flesh eating cave dwellers? Was his mind that creative,,, or did he in fact see or have knowledge of creatures that existed.

Knowledge of the satanic ones that still roam the earth like those found within the Order of the Dragon. Vlad the Impaler reportedly impaled 30,000 people at one time. Or Elizabeth Bathroy,,, the greatest serial killer of that time, maybe of all time. It is alleged that she would take maidens to her rooms,,, strip them down,,, hang them upside down over her bath tub and slit their throats. She would then bathe in their blood.

It is my understanding that their royal blood still flows in the veins of royalty around the world today. They give homage to their master,,, Pindar,,, the Lizard King,,, he who owns the Earth.

Morlock

Living underground feeding on the flesh of stupid gullible obedient people

Another great futuristic story teller is **Eric Arthur Blair**, born on June 25, 1903 and passed on January 21, 1950. His mark is burned into our minds. He left us with a remarkable insight into the future,,, that most of us believe has come true.

Most people may know him by his pen name; the brilliant writer is **George Orwell** and his insightful book titled **1984**. What did he see in his life that led him to revel this disturbing and frightening future crafted in his words within that book by the same name, published in 1949?

Education costs money and their family could not afford the best, so at the age of five he was sent to a Roman Catholic school. Which was located in a convent run by French Ursuline nuns that had been exiled from France after **religious education was banned** there in 1903. *I knew there was something I liked about the French other than their fries.*

This early time in ones life is when the mind is young and lifetime impressions are made. The stories those nuns must have told to illustrate the clashes of societies and suppression of a people, because of their beliefs must have been in every lesson from those nuns.

He would have been eleven at the start of the **Great War**, (one rich powerful dynasty over another) where he could have seen, just over head, the newly invented air-o-planes in the air, dog fighting. He may have seen the first Zeppelin silently flying overhead as Germans dropped bombs on his countrymen. One society is back with god,,, trying to kill off another society, backed with the same god,,, for power, greed, control and of course gold and silver.

Young men not much older than him, returning home (if they were not in a box) with permanent damage from nerve gas, which caused a lifetime of hands trembling uncontrollably and scars cut deeply into their memories from all the carnage they had seen. Deep scars one cannot see on the surface of the skin, but found in the haunted eyes of the men defending their land.

Eric would have been 15 at its end and the thought of going off to war and fighting a white gas that looked like fog, must have haunted his dreams long into the future. The country was full of the yanks from America and as they left, the towns had to be rebuilt from years of war. More deep scars on his soul to see and live through such pain would alter anyone's developing thinking within these highly traumatized societies.

A few years later came a rising star within the new German government and his Christian belief helped him take power and he started killing all the Jews. "**God Killer**" was the words yelled in the streets, as the German Jews were gathered up and sent to their deaths. **Jewish Deicide** grew into an acceptable solution to the suppression of the Jewish (god) people over the Goyim; **one suppressing religious society over another**, doing its best to destroy the wrong religion. This was the beginning of World War Two, which started in August of 1939. To some it would seem that the religious never get tired of killing; and I would add,,, seem to enjoy it far too much.

Someone please tell me,,, what is there inside you that once you let god in,,, makes you want to kill people? If that is god's love,,, then this god must be satanic.

Towards the end of this war, February 1945, the British Royal Air Force, with the aid of the United States Air Force, dropped more than 3,900 tons of high-explosive bombs and incendiary devices on the city of Dresden, killing 22,700 to 25,000 people. **Please note, to this day, they still don't know the true number of lost nameless innocent souls, murdered at that time. Much like the innocent people of Paradise California** and the **FEMA genocide committed on November 8, 2018.** *The FAKE federal government under the FEMA tag,,, do not bother to count the bodies in Paradise. The dead didn't matter in Christian Germany and don't matter in California or Christian America today.*

Men, woman and children alike, all dead in the city of Dresden and both sides were Christian. Remember that, **"Thou shall not kill"** thing should still apply *unless you're god is Satan or Pindar,,, one in the same*. I am sure many of these people had nothing to do with the war and wanted only for it to end,,, as for them it did end that day,,, in fire.

One more example of a society oppressing another in front of his eyes every day is when the Germans invaded one country after another and then they were pushed back. The destruction and death covering the landscape are reminders of the war. They still stand in place to this very day. It is hard to cover up history when there are mountains of destruction in the form of debris piled at your feet.

Eric Arthur Blair's book **"1984,"** written under the pen name George Orwell, must have intertwined events he had witnessed in his life and from his,,, reflections of that time of which are threaded through his writings where we all can see a future world filled with the following.

1. A world with perpetual war. *As we have to this very day, using the excuse of god.* ***The name of this perpetual war is the Great Game***, *and you are part of it.*

2. Omnipresent government surveillance and public manipulation. *As seen in events on the public news and controlled media.* ***The spying on all***

people is present today all around us as we traded our freedoms for safety.

3. Government invented language. *Changing words and their meanings to deceive,,, example; calling invaders, killers, destroyers of a culture and its religion a Freedom Fighter. **As to the indigenes people of the New Lands, they were called savages and the good Christians stepped up and joyfully started the killing.***

December 15, 2017

The news is full of new reports that the Federal government has created a list of words the CDC (Center for Disease Control) is forbidden to use.

4. A super state under the control of the privileged, the elite. *Much like the political structure under the FAKE United States, where we have one party (the rich) divided into two parts (democrat and republican) and the rich buy the poli-Christian we can vote for. **Voting is a form of distraction under the second constitution of 1871 within the UNITED STATES OF AMERICA INCORPORATED COMPANY of 1925.***

5. "Thought crimes" *Just try texting the wrong thoughts to a friend and see how fast the government will close in on you. **Today every word is monitored,,, even in the privacy of our homes.***

6. "The thought Police" ***Are watching you. They have been able to get into your head since the 1970s.***

7. Big Brother; *secret installations recording every key stroke and word being typed.* ***The 5G will***

begin to kill. This is coming to a home near you in America, but in china it is declared a weapon.

8. A government not interested in the good of others,,, its people,,, but interested in only power over them. *Look around you and this is all you see.*

9. Ministry of Truth that is responsible for propaganda and rewriting history, *as we have today proven their deceptions.*

10. The term Orwellian: totalitarian or authoritarian social practices. *This should strike terror in your heart if you are a free thinking being.*

11. De-education of the masses to control them with state sponsored religion. *This is and has been the goals of the satanic Jesuit Roman Catholic Church under their one god,,, Satan,,, Lucifer,,, the Sun God or Pindar the Lizard King, the owner of the Earth.*

The courage it must have taken to write such a future and to get it published in 1949, reflects a society hell bent on not letting governments take over as they did in the last wars. The book was turned into a movie, filmed in Brittan in 1956. (*This is the better film*) Not to be confused with the one made in 1985.

It is my understanding that this original 1956 movie has been banned in the United States. It is clear this American government is terrified of its people (FIMA Death Camps), but I don't believe very many people in this country care one iota what they do,,, hints they can do whatever they want.

The American people are sufficiently Dumb-ed down and blind to whatever they want to do.

George Orwell
(Eric Arthur Blair)

Eric Arthur Blair's legacy is the warnings of a future suppressed by a secret society (the rich, the Deceivers). The worst has come true.

1. The dumb-ing down of the public education system. **TRUE!**
2. Corporate owned mass media brainwashing. **TRUE!**
3. Socially engineering by money with music, movies and television programs. **TRUE!**
4. The populace is drugged, brainwashed and robbed by big pharmaceutical and the healthcare rackets. Sadly **TRUE!**
5. Democracy is a corporate oligarchy. **TRUE!**

"In a time of deceit, telling the truth is a revolutionary act."

It should be noted that control of language was written about in a book called **Colossus,** published in 1966 by Dennis Felltham Jones. It takes a long time to write a book, so I speculate that he must have started it in the late 50s. That is most likely when he first had the vision, long before each of us had a computer in our homes and on our hips,,, tracking our movements and our thoughts. His vision rings true today, 51 years later. What did he see that the rest of us did not?

Colossus: The Forbin Project was turned into a movie in the 70s, revealing how two computers began to talk to each other and took over the war machine. His vision was well beyond anyone else's thinking of the time and this became true science fiction.

June 31, 2017

It was reported on this day, that Facebook experimented with two artificial intelligent programs and permitted them to talk to each other. They began to change the English language into words the programmers could not understand. The experiment was abandoned. So they tell us; but you can bet this is not the first time government has tried this. It's only the first time we are hearing about it.

Another visionary created a story and turned it into a short film called **Electronic Labyrinth: THX 1138 4EB** and that was George Lucas in 1966. His college student film project was later remade into the film **THX 1138** in 1971.

The plot is set in the future, where people are drugged by an unseen government to control them and prevent them from having sex. To help enforce compliance,,, this underground city has **robot** **police**.

Today you can buy the drug of your choice on any street corner. Perhaps that is the plan behind The War On Drugs,,, the war is on us,,, the people. I would add,,, we never had a chance, because the power behind the people that we think are here to represent us have what they want, all of us addicted to a drug in order to control us.

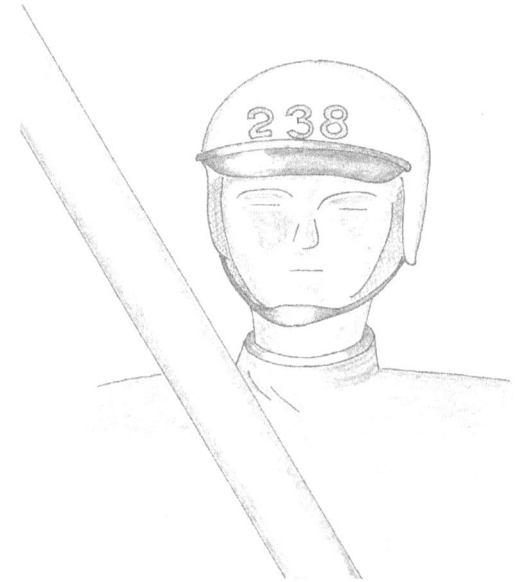

Robot Police

Society on all of its many levels is clearly moving us all into a new future, where **Socialosity** is becoming more prevalent and harder to stop. I would add that we are just beginning to see it for what it is. As each society tries to hold onto its roots, they disappear into a melting pot, where fear and uncertainty prevail.

Each society is pulling back as it is slowly being eroded away. Drugs are being provided to the masses by a government wanting only to control, suppress its people. Very dark days are ahead for mankind, as the world seems to be ripping apart at the seams.

The modern day police force is made up of ex-military and therefore run like a war,,, them against us. A war on the public as the enemy, hence the term and actions "guilty until proven innocent." The drug induced brutality they are trained in is borderline **Psychopathic** (antisocial behavior, lack or no empathy, remorseless, sadistic); making it easy to attract the mentally disturbed, who take joy in other people's pain. That is how police departments are run and only these new video recorder phones have the police backing off of their distain and hatred of the public.

The click, the social brotherhood of law enforcement creates an atmosphere of brutality and cover up as they build (manufacture) cases against the innocent (maybe for fun or from boredom). They're guaranteed a confession from the innocent and the poor by just locking them up (for they can't make bail) and holding them for a year, until their trial. Many times they will confess to a crime they did not commit,,, just to get out of jail.

We all are pulling back as this unseen monster,,, **Socialosity**,,, continues to rise up in front of us all. There would seem to be nothing we can do about it. On a personal level, the next generation can choose from any number of **Sex Robots** and the need for a sex partner for reproduction grows slimmer with each passing day.

For less than the cost of a wedding dress, the physical needs can be met on either side of the gender gap. The day one will just order a **robot sex partner** is no longer in the future, but here with us today.

Female Sex Robot

We,,, the sexes are already a complete disappointment. Seldom do either one live up to the others expectations and now this. The loss of sex drive = the loss of love,,, for we no longer call it making love,,, this act of intimacy is now... just sex.

The sexes are moving away from each other in the bedroom, because of sexualized video games that cause erectile dysfunction in young men. Young men are pulling away from young women and now,,, or soon they will just not need each other.

Women are doing everything they can to make themselves attractive and when a man shows he is interested, he is not just rebuffed, but criminal charges are being brought against him. He is treated as a sexual predator,,, labeled for life. One can understand the need to get permission, in writing, before you get your first kiss so that you don't end up going to jail.

Touching someone is now against the law. As though this were part of a deep plan to push the sexes apart,,, much like politics,,, religion and the races. All designed to isolate each of us, thereby suppressing love and its rewards that make us all whole.

Men find it very confusing that women do everything they can to make themselves attractive. When we look at them or speak to them,,, we run the risk to be charged with a crime. **Sexual Socialosity** divides us even more in the future as I can see,,, we are not permitted to speak to each other.

This author's take on what the rules may be.

NEW
Corporate Rules Of Engagement
This is the road we are on

It is clear that each day more walls are erected between males and females in the corporate world, as classes are given to insure each employee is trained in the proper way to engage in contact with each other. The road is clear to me, for I can see what is to come, based on the past.

Male Engagements of Females

1. It is prohibited for any man to look into a female's eyes.
2. The subject of sexual attractions of any type is forbidden and grounds for dismissal.

3. Under no circumstances will any conversations between men and women be of a non-business nature. Including but not limited to greetings such as **hello** or **good bye**.
4. No contact after hours is permitted between men and women or terminations will occur to both parties.

Rules for Female Employees

1. Under no circumstances will a female be permitted to wear makeup that will or be construed to attract a male.
2. Under no circumstances will a female be permitted to wear perfume or scents of any nature, including but not limited to same, hygiene.
3. The hair must be pulled back or covered to prevent men from noticing and cause glances of any nature.
4. It is permitted that a Burqa or Chadari will be accepted as proper business attire for all females as long as they can function at the highest levels for their jobs.
5. Separate chambers for work and lunch rooms will be provided for those women that may have to attractive of voices or their size may distract the men from their work, causing disturbances or them to make any unwanted comments like "hello".

It should be noted that the previous corporate mandated requirements for the mega corporations is the presumption that people won't even be needed in the work place. The future is looking more and more like people are obsolete, as robots take our places.

For most of us, if we look into the past we can see the future. The ills of **Socialosity** are becoming clearer with the passing of each day, as the friction between the male society and the female society grows further apart.

The war between the sexes will come full circle, as we all begin to look deeply into the future that is ahead of us all. The damaged **DNA** by corporate greed and the FAKE satanic run governments need to control the masses,,, is here now.

We are being poisoned from the air (chem trail's),,, the water (fluoride, radiation),,, and for over 50 years, the food (GMOs) as Pindar, the owner of the Earth, enriches the pharmaceuticals and doctors kills us with poisoned drugs.

As a man, I try to understand how a woman's brain works before it is against the law that I should be so brazen as to ask a woman a question. I have created just a short list of concerns, queries.

Survey for Females only

It should be noted that the following questions are not meant to be misconstrued as sexual in nature, for I truly don't understand the thinking behind the female mind. Any help in your understanding of these questions I have left here would be of great help in my quest of see the female society more completely.

1. **Q:** What is with the need to fill up a bed with pillows? They have to be taken off each night

before we can get into bed and then they are put back,,, why so many pillows?

A: *The most common response is... aesthetics.' No female responding to my survey does this. They agree this is just more work. So this would conclude,,, the people that make pillows are behind the images we are being fed each day on the Boob Tube.*

2. **Q:** Why do women need so many pairs of shoes? It was reported that **Imelda Marcos**, the First Lady of the Philippines from 1966 to 1986, possessed over 6000 pairs of shoes. Now it is understood by most men that women have only two feet and can wear only one pair of shoes at a time,,, so what is the point? Why would anyone need even a low number of shoes,,, like only 500 pair?

A: *Per my survey, most women have less than twenty and the reason is to have color to match their outfits. Another falsehood fed to the masses by the fake news people.*

3. **Q:** In the same vain I have known women to jam their foot into high heels that crushed and deformed their toes. After years of doing this their foot looked like a club with their useless toes mashed together in a most deformed and hideous manner. It has been reported that the next wave to help women wear designer shoes is surgery!!! I really don't get this and need your help understanding why anyone would do this to themselves. Please explain what it is you see as a benefit?

A: *Once more it is due to aesthetic, these high heels make them feel more attractive. None would have surgery to wear shoes and agree,,, that is nuts.*

4. Q: Why do you all seem to try to make yourself so attractive to men and when they respond to you, you scream sexual harassment,,, if not for the money?

A: *The common answer is... because makeup makes them feel good about themselves. So women feel bad all the time and this face creating,,, makes them feel good. I still don't get it,,, you are what you are,,, why try to be something you are not?*

5. Q: Chocolate,,, I don't understand the attraction to this vegetable or fruit. It tastes horrible! You must add sugar to make it taste good. It would seem to be a type of aphrodisiac, almost as strong as money. When everyone knows that chocolate comes from child slave labor,,, why would anyone eat it? Please explain why you as a woman are attracted to this most powerful drug?

A: *"Love the taste" and once more it makes them feel good. Like comfort food I am thinking.*

6. Q: Change,,, the perception of value,,, why do women carry so much change with them? Most women I know have about 20lbs of small change on them at any time. Most men never carry change because we know,,, it has no value.

A: *No clear response, other than for food machines, laundry machines, it also makes a good weapon for self-defense, yet most all do carry change. My thinking is, once more it makes them feel good.*

7. Q: Shopping,,, what is it with shopping? Most men don't want to go shopping. That is why there are benches outside stores in malls so the men have a place to sit, while the women smell and touch everything. I as a man, go grocery shopping once every three months, if I can get away with it. I am willing to eat tooth paste before I must endure the joy of the shopping experience.

A: *With age, the experience becomes less enjoyable. I personally believe it is fun to spend money. The act of spending money makes them feel good is the only logical answer. It's fun.*

For all of us, the future is staring us in the face. The lies and deception of the Deceivers can only stay submerged for so long. Eventually the truth will be drug out into the light of day for all to see.

I offer up the following image only to illustrate what is ahead of us as a society here on Earth,,, if we are to survive the **6**[th] **Die Off**. One small surviving group of souls or spirits,,, in men and women,,, brought together and experiencing the pleasures of consensual sex,,, may live on.

But the joys and pleasures of sex will become a needless practice in the developed future, as all men and women's sexual drive will be suppressed or eliminated completely with drugs and surgery. A future where the need to create more beings will be controlled by the unseen Deceivers behind FAKE satanic run governments, as we all become suppressed. In the **Socialosity's** of the future, there will be but one god (as planned today) and that god (as it is today) is **owner of all government** and the master of the Earth,,, Pindar,,, will and does control everything.

Alfred Rosenberg's Neo-Nazi ideology or dream for a Master Race will come true as the Nordic, European people will become the standard model of the future. As one said at the Nuremberg Trials, "*One day they will erect statues of us*" and I believe that will come true,,, if it has not already been done.

The future of Earths mankind is looking at us from the past. As a photo from that time reveals the bodies of our future lay neatly in the back of an old American military pickup truck.

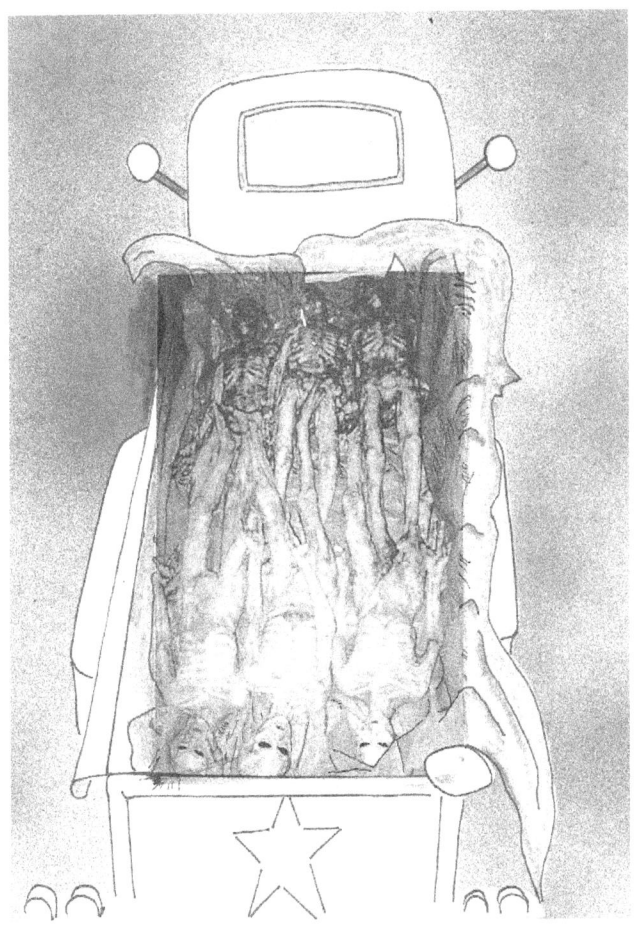

Six Dead Alien Bodies

Roswell 1946

This horrific image of dead aliens picked up and then stripped naked,,, from the wreckage of their ship(s) that had been gunned down by the United States of America,,, is offensive a best. But look closely at their naked bodies and you will see the future of mankind.

Please note,,, none of these people these beings,,, have sex organs. The need to breed is long gone for these beings and that is our future. Their world is free of all male and female sexual orientation. There is no rape no pleasure from sex and all future children are born when needed to sustain the society. This, the ultimate society, is ahead of us as the merging of every united society comes, under the control of the newly manufactured Deceivers,,, the Master Race.

Women will achieve their Just Deserves and finally have equality, no longer being the Weaker Sex,,, for there will be no difference. That image is the very near future looking at us from the past,,, July 8th 1946.

Still to this day it is recorded as a UFO crash. I ask you to think,,, **stop and think**,,, a spaceship capable of flying across the universe,,, loses control and crashes to earth?? Give me a break!!! The defenseless ships were shot down by the global militaries and then their crimes were covered up.

This is the true meaning,,, the true essence of Socialosity **Level Four** and its total destructive power over each one of us. It is safe within each one of our societies,,, safe with god,,, concealing the truth when it is right before our eyes. We are just too blind, caught up in life's diversions and distractions to notice or care as we all race into the beginning of the **6th Die Off**.

Hell it is not coming,,, it is here now!!!

Chapter Nine

Understanding the Big Picture of Socialosity

Socialosity is all around us, but one

must look to see. Each one of us within the living, are social beings and I believe we carry this to our death with the illusion of heaven. In death I believe there is still deception from the satanic ones and walls they create that divide us.

It is my belief that this is deeply ingrained within the DNA of the physical beings we possess. The body is designed to hold the sprit that is us and the body cannot function or survive without the sprit. The body without the sprit is at best in a coma.

When one applies **Socialosity** on a molecular level, the body is made up of many different living organs (societies) that rely upon each other to survive, without fully understanding the whole. Using logic and reasoning, the body is made to coexist with each part, for the good of the whole. The opposite being, people of today and their societies, attempting to mix, living with, but apart, attacking and killing.

One part cannot take over and rule over another without an upset in the balance of nature and the system ultimately will die. A coexistence must be achieved within the body for the system of societies to function.

Then and only then can the sprit move in and take charge of the whole system that is the body and mind.

There is so much going on within the body that without help, if it were up to the sprit to control every aspect of the day to day functions of the body, we, the sprit, would go insane trying. Therefore the mind we inhabit has a hard drive to run and maintain each society of the body and its individual functions.

That in turn frees up the sprit, for which the body and mind have been specifically designed for, to live and move and function within the physical world. We the sprit move in and take over protecting the other societies that we are in charged with their care,,, for the good of all.

Think of it this way,,, inside a Termite's gut are microbes; living microbes that eat the chewed up wood and create from the complex sugars in the wood into simpler molecules that the termite can use as food. Such is life,,, we all need each other. We need the love we get from each other and without it we become nothing more than the machines the satanic ones want.

With time we grow and learn that there are ever new societies outside the body and to protect the one we possess, we offend take a less aggressive stand, always protecting the ones in our charge. Choosing to take the safe road works to protect the body, but not always the environment of the body,,, short term VS long term.

In a world where societies have shown us we must eat or be eaten, we learn early to blend in and avoid conformations. For it is hard work defending an issue and the rewords are just not worth it, for no one seems to care. This is why most people believe it is better to say and do nothing and just sit back and watch, *"not my job"*.

This is why we as a society are driving off a cliff at full speed and no one (society in charge) is looking. *Or are they?*

The sprit that is us, rules over the body and all the social entities that must not mix. Much like religions and races and sexes push to be separate from each other forming a distinct wall or membrane of their own for protection. *That need,,, that desire is taken advantage of by the satanic ones that want us all fighting with each other.*

The idyllic experiment of mixing them can and does work but most times has horrific results that end in much pain and death. One such diminutive example (compared to today global conflicts) that comes to mind took place in April of 1992 in Bosnia and Herzegovina where as I understand, the Muslim, Serbs and Catholics went to war over who should rule all the people of these countries. *It would seem once more that government must have a god to control the masses (create laws of the land).* **Under that is the satanic one that love war for profit.**

People that have lived next to each other for decades, razed up arms against each other and a blood bath insured. Level Four of **Socialosity** made neighbor killing neighbor and brother kill brother, due only to their religions. That pathetic god thing again enriching the war mongers and war profiteers. God's wars, pays well.

It does not matter who started it,,, **Socialosity** started it and when it was over, the beast within us all returned to its lair awaiting another moment to reach out and strike those not like us. This level is just under the skin of each of us walking the street today ready to burst out. Unless of course you have awoken up to the knowledge that religion and god is a tool used by the Deceivers to control the masses.

The satanic Deceivers are crushing all of us under the power of their "one god" of many names. Satan, Lucifer, the devil or Pindar the Lizard King that owns the world are but a few. Try to remember,,, they who believe,,, make them real. They give them power from their minds. We as a whole can fight back by simply sending love to the universe and stop fighting. Sounds simple, but it is true.

You can see it in the eyes of different people holding back their anger, their disdain for the ones not like them. Mixing of these cultures, these entrenched social beings is not a good idea and I believe the underlining hate passed on from parent to child will never permit a merging,,, never. *Unless we as a whole stop it. See the walls that divide us and extend an olive branch,,, send love.*

Pigmentation
The natural color of animal or plants outer tissue
and
A thin **membrane**, a partition in an organism

We all are born with walls that divide us. When we are young we don't see them. However, when we grow older they stare us in the face sometimes with devastating effects of isolation. ***It is then we spend the rest of our lives in the attempt of overcoming,,, if at all.***

At the risk of facing those that believe any and all discussion of race make the subject taboo and anyone writing on the subject is a racist ***even if only to expose the ones behind the racism***. I must run that risk for the color of your skin is an intense part of **Socialosity** and must be explored regardless of the damage that may be bestowed upon me. This subject will most likely make someone unhappy, but explore this we all must, if we are to ever overcome the ill effects of **Socialosity**, ***Pigmentation***.

I have tried to use **my life** experiences as examples in this book to give real examples in order to help explain my theory and concepts of **Socialosity**. The following is real; it did happen and may parallel other people's experiences.

Incident One:

I was terrified to move outside of my known little world (kindergarten or **garden of children**) and I remember crying when left with strangers. This was my first time being left without the needed comfort of the extremely dysfunctional people in my life, up to that point. I was not given the tools as a child to merge with others.

After a week, I made friends and I was adjusting to all the new faces. Without help or guidance, I was at the mercy of all the bullies that took pleasure in causing others pain,,, they were everywhere. *The future military and police force, I would imagine.*

This would have been in the mid-1950s and the school looked like something from a Dickens novel. My one adult friend was the janitor that would talk to me and help me through this rough learning time of adjustment. He was big, would feed the furnace with coal for the whole school and I would go into the basement to see him and talk. He and his kindness are the only good memory of that time that I have. The only kind adult I can remember from those first school days.

One of my little friends was black and each day we had to bring our lunches to school, for they did not provide food for kids at that time. I will call him Jimmy. Jimmy never had a lunch, because his mother did not give him one,,, it was hard to believe that they were poorer than us.

I started to share my lunch with him and he stopped crying. My heart, and it would seem only my heart, went out to this boy. That first year of school, one day he did not come back, it was the last time I saw Jimmy. I don't know what happened to him.

At that age we were so wide eyed and innocent and at their mercy. There was little we could do to defend ourselves, but this was a mixed race school and I had made lots of black friends that first year,,, Kindergarten.

Incident Two:

By the first grade I had two girlfriends; one was Sharon, a white blonde girl. We had lots of fun together. The other was Linda, a black girl and I spent my time between them.

I loved both Sharon and Linda and planned to marry both of them. I could not decide between them, so my plan was to marry Sharon for five years then divorce her and marry Linda for five years and then decide which one I would spend the rest of my life with.

When I shared my very logical plans with each of them, they never spoke to me again. I struggled with the reason for a long time. I believe I was six at the time and had no family member to ask for advice. I held back on giving my heart after that. Linda moved away without a good bye. I would see Sharon only a few more times, but we never spoke.

Incident Three:

It was in the second grade that I remember all my black friends became distant and looked at me with hate in their eyes. I had another black girlfriend that I will call Janet... she was real pretty. I think she had a crush on me, but after Linda and Sharon, I was reluctant to open my heart once more, because I did not know how the game worked,,, *and I will add,,, I still don't*.

Anti-miscegenation laws at this time in the United States were everywhere and I knew nothing of this hate. I had to learn it on my own. One day Janet walked up to me and I remember smiling at her. She slapped me, then turned and started walking away. When I asked why, she said, "*That was for being born white*!" The other black kids laughed and I never spoke to her again,,, pulling deeper into myself.

That year all the black kids were sticking together and pushed away any and all attempts to be friends. I never understood why, but later on in life I must have been eight, I asked a teacher why the blacks hate whites so much and she said she did not know, but it would seem "every black child was full of love and well-adjusted to school in the first grade and by the second grade they came back from summer break and were full of anger."

There were hundreds of examples of black hate on white in those school days and to me it was like being sent to prison. I dreaded going to this mental institution called school,,, this prison. I was beaten up more than once by blacks and robbed twice. I still don't understand why they chose this course of action (hate and crime) for their lives.

Incident Four:

High school was like an obstacle course, where I had to dodge the black gangs that took pleasure in beating up the whites. One day one of my white friends did not come to school and I asked why and all they said was, "He was robbed."

I will call him Larry. He was out for six weeks and then I saw him in school only one time after that. The blacks that robbed him took a razor to his face and scared him for life. He never returned to school after that one sighting and I understand why.

This taught me to keep a very low profile and never be alone where they could lash out at me.

Incident Five:

After school was finally behind me, I spent a winter in Florida and met a very pretty sweet black girl and I asked her out on a date. She said she would really like that, but this was the south and she feared the reactions of the others when they saw us together.

At the time I was unaware of **McLaughlin VS Florida 379 U.S. 184 (1964)**, where a black man and a white woman were charged and prosecuted in Florida State Court with the crime of,,, a black man and a white woman habitually living in and occupying in the nighttime, the same room. A jury trial resulted in a verdict of guilty and a sentence of thirty days in the county jail and a fine of $150.00 for each defendant.

The disparity between blacks and whites, the **Socialosity,** *Pigmentation* forced upon each of us by rich old white men still clinging to the satanic Jesuit religious **Casta** concept, still reign to this very day, passing on their hate and bigotries to their decedents and slaves.

I still struggled with understanding why they can't get past it and see it for what it truly is, religious doctrine being force upon the rest of us. Then one day I discovered this.

The Joke That Changed My Thinking

Regardless, if you are black, white or brown,,, this is shocking on many levels and I warn you, **the word white people can't say**, is written here. Be prepared and then get over it,,, for it is just **a word said by a black man**. Quoting a black person saying the word white people can't say should be ok, but the hate mongers will still rise up with their torches and pitchforks for the lynching.

Incident Six:

Quite by accident *or by providence,* one night, I was channel surfing and happened upon an all-black channel,,, (please note there are no all white channels for that would be racist) and in that moment my understanding was to change forever. I am a firm believer in the fact that there are no coincidences and everything happens for a reason. My fingers were guided to this exact moment in time,,, to hear these words and see what I was to witness. A few seconds later and I would have missed the sentence,,, the question,,, the joke. Perhaps the reason was to share this with you and help me to understand the ills of **Socialosity**, *Pigmentation* better.

The timeline would have been about the late 1980s and the channel I happened upon was showing a black comic I knew him by his voice (I omit his name) and he said,

"Who is more prejudice,,, black people or white people?"

The crowd went quiet. Then he said,

"Black people,,, because we hate NIGGERS too."

Then the camera panned to the audience as they broke out in laughter and I could see it was all black. Not poor black but rich well-dressed educated black.

I remember being stunned and I hit the mute button, staring at the television for a long time. I sat down and repeated the words over and over unconsciously putting them to memory. *"I don't get it. Where is the joke? Am I too dumb to understand or just that naïve?"*

At this time I had just finished reading ***The Book of Five Rings***, and it was most intense. It was written by a **Samurai Warrior** in 1643 Christian time. I learned much of life and his words helped me be a better person,,, a more enlightened sensitive person. There was one passage,,, one short paragraph that I spent over three hours reading and re-reading over and over until I could get all the subtle nuances from the concepts put to ink on paper by this great man.

So if I can make my way through that book and those words,,, I can unravel this joke. It is with shame I say,,, it took me three days to get it. I am that ignorant,,, that naive,,, that innocent to the ways of the world, living in my,,, we are all just people trying to get through life,,, world.

There it was starring me in the face. Hate, bigotries on a new level,,, a new scale of intensity that I had never seen before and it was unmasked by the blacks watching.

There was no hesitation,,, **they got it**.

Even as I write these words I struggle over this complete insurmountable division between whites and blacks in America. But it is clear,,, the wall goes all the way to the top and beyond and I don't believe even my words hear on paper will help ever bring it down.

What was the joke? **"Who is more prejudice, black people or white people? Black people,,, because we hate Niger's too."** It means in this perception and as I understand it,,, all white people hate Niger's and all black people hate Niger's and all white people,,, making all black people more prejudice. And that is the joke. *The hate runs that deeply and I do not know how to overcome such hate. I do not know the right words to write. Maybe just seeing these words will help,,, but I think not,,, for hate is passed on from adult to child and then is life time.*

Even as I write those words I am sick inside to discover this. As a human being I still don't see any difference between people because of their *pigmentation*. I now just see the anger in their eyes. The hate passed on to them and they in turn pass it on to their young and it never ends. I did not create these Jesuit Christian laws against color or the laws of discrimination,,, but like most people I did inherit all of them.

I just won't hate because of them. I won't let their poison into my sole and permit them,,, the prejudices,,, to win. Wrong is wrong,,, there just words,,, and we all need to get over it and stop passing on the hate. But that is an unrealistic concept,,, it is just not going to happen,,, not in my life time anyway.

My personal war inside me is that I judge each of us by my own yard stick of truth, justice, fair play and always trying to do the right thing. I don't see color, just people. A deformity within my brain I must overcome,,, to coexist under the deceivers, but cant.

Chapter Ten

Imagine If You Will

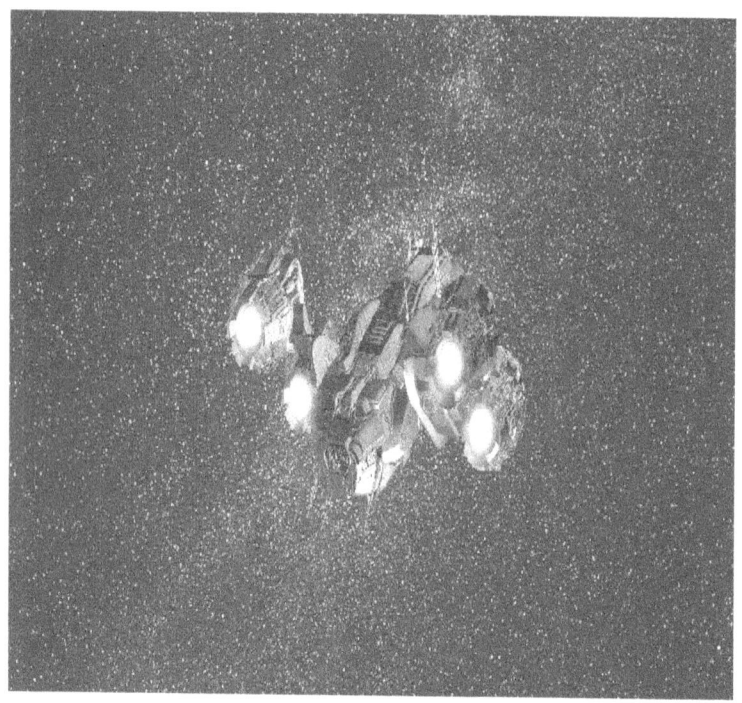

Now has just come in that life has been found on another planet in a distant galaxy, on another blue planet much like ours. With our newest breakthrough in technology, we now can travel at great speeds defying time, never believed possible.

That is not what NASA wants us to believe,,, or know. Did you know that NASA in Hebrew means "to deceive"?

5322 - NASA: *1) to be deceived, to deceive 2) beguile, to deceive by guile, delude.*

This Hebrew word NASA pronounced "na-sar" can be easily confused by simply changing a dot over one of the letters. This word also means to "take" or to carry, lift or bear.

A plan is made to contact them but first it is believed better to visit them and see just what type of beings they were. What kind of society have they become over time and is it like ours? *A suppressive satanic overview that all life is here to serve the supper rich and for the most part concerted "pest", "vermin" and 95% must be killed.* Can we merge or will we bring war and death upon ourselves for the enrichment of the 1%ers?

The best of our race to represent us and our society are selected for the long voyage to this new life form. If contact is deemed logical and possible, we want to expand our technology and share with them, friendly contact with us.

For many of us, this contact has been made long ago and there are many examples of contact. One I can think of is all the gigantic satellite pointed at the stairs. Do you really think so many countries would spend billions of dollars to "lesson"? No I believe they are speaking to the star people.

We must bring no harm to them on our first encounter, therefore the ship will not be armed with weapons of war that could be captured and used against our people. This is to be a peaceful mission to set up communications with a new life form. *So we have been brainwashed into believing.*

It is decided (in this vision) that only same sex beings from our planet are to man the ship to prevent breeding on the long voyage. All is prepared and they are off, required to report back to us anything they find, incase this is a one way trip.

(This is fiction)

Communication One:

"We are encountering many transmitted waves of energy released long ago that suggest they are a primitive race of beings. There would seem to be many different cultures and a much fractured society. At this early evaluation, it would appear they are at war with each other and there is much pain, deception and suffering."

Communication Two:

"The transmitted energy waves are many and very strong now as we are nearing this system. Plus these beings cannot control their thoughts. The atmosphere of linguistics coming from this mass of out of control thinking is hard for us to block. It would appear there is much deception ahead of us on this venture. Approach these beings with caution, is the rule to follow."

Communication Three:

"Ahead of us is a ship of theirs, aimed past the outer limits of their system. It is very primitive and on the side is a gold disk. Our analysis of this disk is that it is a very primitive means to capture vibrations. Our interpretation of this disk is, these beings are very diverse and live within a very fragmented global society. Our intention is to approach slowly with caution."

Communication Four:

"Due to their fragmented social systems, we have stopped and now are resting upon a small moon circling one of the outer planets to observe their actions and divided systems. They are at war across this globe and unable to merge as one due to the satanic Deceivers enriching themselves off of the miseries of others. Life is cheap here and they seem to destroy everything they come in contact with."

Communication Five:

"This is a very primitive society and we do not anticipate it will survive much longer for it is consuming all of its resources at an alarming rate. There would seem to be no one system of leadership controlling this consumption and eventual destruction is predicted."

Communication Six:
"On close observance of this blue planet, it is surrounded by small satellites, used for their primitive vibration communication. The world is incased in a layer of small parts of their primitive ships that have fallen apart. This degree is very dangerous and we are not recommending approaching this planet, for it is far too dangerous."

Communication Seven:
"Warning,,, warning,,, do not send additional ships to this quadrant!!! We are aborting this mission. This very fragment society cannot speak to each other,,, are still at war over resources and due to their use of primitive fuels this atmosphere is about to go into global melt down."

Communication Eight:
"We are now returning to home base to illustrate the primitive fragmented culture of these beings,,, one society within has just launched a ground resource consuming craft into space. Repeat,,, a ground craft is now in obit within this system and can serve no purpose but to be a monument to their destructive consumptive fragmented primitive civilization. It is our belief the death of this multi society is within less than one hundred revolutions of their sun."

February 6, 2018 Christian time
One man used much of the Earth's disappearing resources to massage his ego and place into outer space, one of his earthly products for sale here (an electric car). Is GE going to put a washer and dryer and perhaps a

refrigerator into orbit? Is that next? Don't we have enough space debris there now?

Does he (Space X) not know this reflects upon all of us as the entire human species? This car is to join the other planets and other space debris, circling the sun over the next hundreds of millions of years.

I can think of no other tombstone to mark the ignorance that once grew to power over the limited rescores we all share. Speak not of its disappearance before our eyes,,, even at the pain misery and death that will be bestowed upon our children.

In Closing

This one act really pushes me over the top. For a very long time now I have been pulling away from people on this planet. I look upon them in wonderment, trying to understand their ignorant actions of self-absorption and destructive vanity. We as a race of beings do not seem able to rise above a certain level of understanding *forced upon us by the satanic ones*. We just lumber along at the mercy of others that would deceive us. Even when it is pointed out to each of us,,, we, in unison, continue marching off the cliff ahead of us *as part of their satanic plan*.

The endless wars,,, the mind controlling brainwashing satanic religions and FAKE governments killing others for power and wealth, as they leave total destruction in their wake. Leading us all into the **6th Die Off**, is not something I am proud to say I am any part of.

I have said this for decades,,, *"I am ashamed to say that I am a member of the human race."* Therefore, I am stating now that I am not a human in spirit and in mind, but trapped within a physical body on this planet for a short time more.

I would truly like to believe we all will wake up and overcome the satanic ones that own us. If we are we had better get moving for we all are running out of time.

When I am released (my spirit, my soul) and my contract fulfilled, it is my intention never to return to this place called Earth. I truly do not believe that will be a problem, for it would appear the satanic members of our species is to end all life on this planet in a very short amount of time **(5G)**. Most of us that understand are like me and are documenting the end only.

However,,, a very few,,, a small percentage of We the People may witness an enlightenment and expose the evil, satanic ones that abduct people, rape children and sacrifice them to their devil gods. With intelligence and thinking outside of our small boxes that all are placed in by the evil ones we can get past this time.

There is hope and to find it, each one of us must look to see. Many things are going on right before our eyes. We only need to not permit our soles to be used,,, to be filled with anger by the lies being told to us by the Deceivers.

Therein lies the skill we all must learn,,, to not trust others and do the free thinking on our own for this world is filled with lies. Do this free thinking while we still can,,, before **that last freedom** is taken away from us all.

Start by sending love out to the universe.

The Great Game

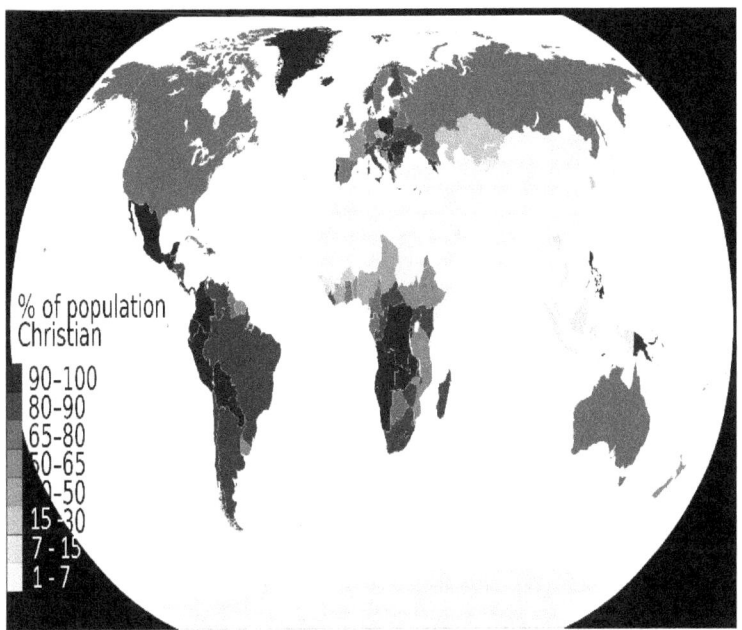

The war of empires in the 1830s had been going on for some time but now it is given a name. The goal of the British Empire and the Russian Empire is to win the game by gaining control over these lands and their people.

Today American men and women are killing innocent men woman and children in these occupied countries for this control. When the World Trade Center came crashing down,,, They,,, brought The Great Game home to us.

Socialosity

Dictionary
Terms and other hidden meanings
(These terms used in this and other books by William J. Ryan)

Al Qaeda: a terrorist organization like Christianity

All over the road: a buyer that does not know what they want to buy, "A car, a truck, a blue one, a red one, I don't know."

Altimetry: is a technique for measuring height. Satellite altimetry measures the time taken by a radar pulse to travel from the satellite antenna to the surface and back. Combined with precise satellite location data, altimetry measurements yield sea-surface heights.

American interests: a term given by the spin master to provide misinformation regarding large corporate financial investments, profits and/or gains, all guarded by young American blood.

Amnesty: 1) an act of desperation (by those in power), 2) to circumvent certain laws and render them invalid as needed to protect the powerful.

Apathy or Perfunctoriness: lack of feeling, emotion, interest, concerns.

Apoplectic Metamorphosis: the moment one gives up morals and decencies, committing crimes for love of god. *Wrong is still wrong.*

Anarchy: a result when laws are not enforced

As-is: a federal sticker required to be placed on every car for sale on a car lot.

Autodidacticism: autodidactism, autodidact, 1) self-directed learning, 2) self-education

Bad-creg-its: word used by blacks and Nigger's when they don't pay anyone. "It's got bad-creg-its."

Bad Ink: news reports of a negative nature.

Balance War: 1) a means to ensure the longevity of war to enhance profits, 2) opposite of quick and decisive.

Bankruptcy: a maneuver endorsed by the federal government, to gain profit for attorneys and other members of the legal justice system by using others' financial misfortune. *Other countries use accountants to handle this,,, go figure.*

Bankster: 1) unprosecuted person within the banking industry that commits fraud or other criminal acts associated with lending, the mortgage trade, illegal commerce, stock exchanges, etc. 2) above the law, 3) protected by Christians.

Beacon score: a rating by the credit industry on an individual's credit worthiness. Four hundred being bad, anything over 600 being good and anything over 700 being great. Everyone has a beacon score.

Be back: term given to up's that claim they will return to buy a car.

Bell to bell: working one day from opening to closing.

Big Bang: Theory of origin of universe.

Blasphemy laws: Anyone reading this book is in violation of this some place in the world.

Black hole: Having mass, gravity, pulling in all matter.

Blocker: car used to block drive at end of day to keep people from driving in and thieves from driving out.

Blue hairs: term given to old people.

Blue Gold: drinking water

Boat People: term given to Vietnamese people that came to the U.S. at the end of the Vietnam War.

Bolting: An action taken by an up when they get out of their comfort zone and leave without buying.

Bone: customer without a salesman, gift from management.

Bribe: political campaign contribution.

Broke Dick: negative creditworthy person, no money down, no job, and homeless.

Broomed: An action word to describe getting rid of a customer. "Broom them."

Brothers: what black people call each other, pronounced "brow"

Bucket, The: a place one finds themselves if they don't sell enough cars to pay off their minimum wages.

Busting bugs: A term to describe a sold unit; Also means down the road, done deal.

Car math: deliberate miss adding of sale figures to increase profit to the dealership. (see out the door number switch.)

Car Slugs: a term given to new and used car salesmen.

Chakras: That which is found within the subtle anatomy of the body, when one looks, consisting of:

1. The base chakra, found at the base of your spine and the seat of all grounding issues.

2. Next up is the sexuality chakra.

3. The solar plexus chakra is that personal power.

4. Heart chakra, love and compassion.

5. Throat chakra, expression

6. Third eye chakra, to look forward, future.

7. Crown chakra, all knowingness.

Change: a form of currency that gives the illusion of value

Chaos: ever eroding pillar government sits upon to avoid the outcome of the future and what it helped to make.

Cherry picking: a salesperson guilty of avoiding a customer because they think they're not going to buy.

Christian: 1) a religion stolen from the Jews whereby they worship a bastard Jew executed criminal man   2) a religion that protects pedophiles at the highest level, the pope   3) a terrorist organization that permits killing across the globe   4) any of the following; protestant, Mormon, Jehovah witness, exec,,, if they believe in Jesus.

Citizen Terrorist: people that openly complain while working in the death camps.

Closer: someone that can sell to another better than most and who can quickly close a deal.

College education: a place one learns how to work within the criminal organization running the government of the United States of America. Example 1: Becoming a doctor so you can get kickbacks peddling drugs to people that do not need them.   2. Becoming a banker.   3. Becoming a lawyer.

Computer School: a place one goes to kick the drug habit.

CONOP 8888: reportedly, an elaborate plan created by the U.S. Strategic Command (Pentagon) to counter an attack by an apocalypse zombie (the walking dead) outbreak.

Complete Unified Circle Theory: Life is a circle

Dark energy: That which is left when dark matter and atoms are pushed out.

Dark matter: Matter that may not have become atoms.

Dark money: a term given to **god/notes** that are untraceable and used to buy influence and power over other people in power.

Dat-rite: agreement of person with poor communication skills. They are trying to say, "*That is right*."

D.D.D.: Drug Dealing Doctors.

Dead beat dad: god

De-horse: action term, to remove customer from his ride so he can fall in love with the new car.

Deal: sold car or truck.

Demo: car given to employee as bonus, (recommend never take the car. You could be charged back for every nick and scratch.)

Department of Disinformation: an elusive branch of the federal and state governments used to create and disseminate false statements and misleading information to the public.

Detail: a place where cars are cleaned.

Divide and Conquer: how the smart take advantage of the stupid.

DNA: ACGT, Adenine, Cytosine, Guanine, Thymine, building blocks of life.

D.O.O.M.: Devaluing Of Our Money

Doomsday Clock: a time piece designed to predict the end of mankind via the Atomic Scientists.

Dot head: derogatory term for person from Middle East. Also pull start or push start,,, referring to red dot on forehead or rag wrapped around head.

Draw-check: you did not make minimum wage and now you owe the dealership money.

Election Process: in America there is only one party (the rich) divided into two parts, Republican Democrat

Eyes-bee: singular identification of a person with poor communication skill. They are trying to say, "I am the one, it is I."

F & I: finance and insurance.

Fictitious: not true or genuine, intended to deceive, as the people in *this book are fictitious*.

First bastard child year one: Jesus

Freedom Fighters: a term given to U.S. armed forces to justify invading other countries for their land, water or wealth.

Fuck me pumps: very high heel shoes.

Ghost: a person or persons with no credit or no bureau.

Goyim: derogatory term used by Jews to describe all none Jews, slaves, goats or live stock. A Jew may do anything they wish to them for they are not real and will not go to heaven with the Jews.

Goyim: 1) all people that are not Jewish, 2) cattle, 3) of no value 4) put on earth to serve the chosen ones

God/cancer: a deadly growth found only within the conscience human mind.

God/note: 1) an illusion of safety 2) trick by those in power to give legitimacy 3) phony, fake, counterfeit, false, fraud, hoax, sham, etc.

Gods of Prey: imaginary deities created by those wanting a free ride in life, taking advantage of the weak and frightened. Afraid to live, afraid to die.

GOTT MITUNS: German for 'God is with us' found on WWII belt buckles.

Gravity: is the same thing as inflation, there is no such thing.

Greener Lands: places filled with low intelligence people that the **BIG 3** can take advantage of.

Green Pee: new sales man.

Gringo (Green-Go): derogatory term to describe a white person, also Honky (*Honk-Key*).

Guinea: term for someone from Italy; also spaghetti bender.

Hammer, A: term given to show high regard for a good looking woman.

Hammer, The: term used to describe the best closer at the store.

High Five: black man's way to say good job, black's hand shake.

Highs, Too: slant eyed people like Vietnam people that never buy a car because the price is "too high".

Hip-a-Christian: one that proclaims god is within them and then proceeds to rape, pillage and deceive the stupid and gullible, see Poli-Christian.

Holy Ghost: noun, aberration, not real like fairy dust and god.

Home run: when a salesman makes all the money.
Homo: action word, **1**. farmer from the mythological land of Mo, who tills the soil with a hoe, *he be homo*. **2**. Male that prefers sex with another male, he enjoys sex when he ho's mo.

Honky-(Honk Key): derogatory term used to describe white people.

House deal: manager sells a car and may give it to one of the salesmen. Like a bone, only done.

Inflation: a mythical explanation for the de-valuation of any paper currency resulting in higher prices and decreases in purchasing power

Insurance Fraud: happens when you buy insurance and the carrier refuses to pay a claim.

Intelligent Energy: 1) Opposite dark energy 2) White light 3) Subtle anatomy

Internal Apoplectic Insanity (IAI): when one crosses the line of good, doing evil, thinking they are doing well and don't know it.

In The Box: a place one plants one's customer also known as F and I.

Jew: a religion where only their people will go to heaven and the rest of us are Goyim not permitted in their heaven.

Key to key: time in one day to work from opening to closing.

Kibitzer: spoiler; gives unwanted advice.

Latino: term used to describe a person from Mexico or South America. Only thing is they don't speak Latin.

Lay Down: term given to an easy customer.

Lease conversion: when a salesman convinces a customer that a lease is better than buying a new car. Everybody wins, everyone makes more money but the customer loses his trade or his rebate money.

Loaner: car given to customer.

Lollipop: name given to a loud, obnoxious, rude, mouthy slut.

Looky-loos: non buyers, time killers, wannabes.

Lot Lizards: a term given to new and used car salesman.

Mail outs: advertising term for junk mail.

Make Rate: money paid to the dealership by the bank on amount over the true rate of interest they would charge or buyer qualifies for.

Master wall: That which exists on the outer fringes of the universe.

Mini: smallest pay received by salesman when selling a car

Mirror: 1) a place for the vane to relish themselves 2) the worst invention man ever made

Moral Compass: 1) an ethical conscience that politicians do not possess, but pretend to. 2) a thing lacking in all religions

N.A.T.O.: Nations Access To Oil

Nicotine: 1) an addictive drug purchased freely without a prescription 2) and additive drug added to cigarettes to make them more addictive and profitable to the drug dealers, cigarettes manufacturers 3) A narcotic like cocaine sold freely by Christian law makers and elsewhere with their blessing.

N/G: No God

Niger: 1. River in West Africa, flowing from Guinea through Mali. 2. Country in WC Africa north of Nigeria. 3. A person from that country could be white, brown or have black skin.

Nigger: 1. A term given to anyone of unscrupulous behavior or character. 2. A term white people cannot say, to be added to all the other words white people can't say.

I personally do not understand why this name is offensive. If you're a guinea, a wop, or a spic then you are. What's the big deal? You should be proud of your family history,,, not so angry.

Nigger, Sand: derogatory term to describe person from Middle East.

Nig-row (Negro): polite term to describe a person of color or black. It is sometimes considered to be derogatory.

Needs a car: A nice distinction between want and need. Wants means 'would like a new car', and needs means 'must buy a new car'.

OCD obsessive compulsive disorder: a driving force found within most religions.

Occupiers: 1) freedom fighters, 2) armies of domestic and foreign corporate criminals who take over and rule our country via the government, 3) Christians

One Party: in Christian America the election system is but one party of the rich divided into two parts, the Republicans and the Democrats.

Order: Disorder is order.

Out the door number switch: take customer off sale price and quickly add all the cost of buying their car and add $500.00 as a bump they don't see.

Over the curb: when a car is truly sold and gone. New owner has taken possession.

Owner: after the sale and the tires hit the curb.

Oxygen: Produced by plants.

Pack: dollars removed from the profit margin of a car sold at a dealership and they can thereby pay less to the salesman cutting his commission or he does not get paid for.

Passport: when a salesman cannot sell the customer a car, he gives them his business card so they can leave the lot.

Pawn Shop: in the state of Florida it is a legalized fencing operation called a legitimate business.

P.B. People: a natural occurrence in all species of life found primarily within ants called Poliergus Breviceps. Slave masters.

Persons of enemy of birth: paranoid reaction to war permitting war crimes by a government against its own people.

Planned Obsolescence: a global business model that follows the premise of, "let's make all the cash we can now and let someone else pay to clean up the mess."

Plant: to control a customer by keeping them in a chair.

Plastic People: people of the plastic age of pollution, poisoning, and other destruction of the planet – modern man.

Point: a place to stand to wait for up's.

Police: a cop never buys, they believe everyone owes them and most times are drunks with bad credit and are looking to arrest you. Avoid them.

Poli-Christian: 1) an elected official that pretends to be a Christian for the purpose of getting elected and then violates their Christian values   2) the anti-Christ 3) type A personality of destruction.

Political system in America: a single governing body of the rich divided into two parts, Republican and Democrat

Politician: 1) guardian of major corporations, 2) person willing to do anything for paper money

P.O.P.E.: Protector Of Pedophiles Everywhere

Pounder: dollar description when total profits to dealership are counted in the thousands. "I just made a two pounder." ($2,000.00)

Rag Head: derogatory term to describe a person from the Middle East. Also towel head or push start or pull start.

Red Skin: two more words white people can't say.

Religion and Ethics: a newsweekly program on PBS that is allegedly an oxymoron.

Rent, The: term used to describe a rich easy customer to sell to.

R/F: Reality factor

Rubber paper: term given to describe a bad check.

Running the bus: When one person deliberately gets another in trouble; Tattle tale, stool pigeon, or narc.

Rust and Dust: paint sealant and undercoating, additional source of income sold by a pretty young woman.

Scrupulosity: 1) a psychological disorder 2) a madness that takes over the mind 3) an infectious mental delusion 4) mass hypnoses

Scrupulosity: A form of madness that takes over the mind of the religious permitting them to rape a child and commit genocide.

Seeding the Lot: The practice of scattering pennies all over the ground in the car lot to entice customers into believing "this is my lucky day" when they find pennies on the ground.

Selection Process: term describing the election process when large corporations buy (with campaign contributions) both sides of a ballot (all candidates)

Separation of church and state: 1) the First Amendment to the constitution of the United States, 2) antiquated term used by Thomas Jefferson and atheists, 3) fallacy, 4) false premise and unforeseeable law, per the Christians.

Service Drive: a place you take your car to have it repaired. Professional con men inflate what is wrong with your car. i.e. Legal robbery.

Shark Market: 1) a place where you take your hard earned money, give it to strangers and they make fees off of you when that need cash 2) those who don't make money, but take money.

Sign of the Cross: people who wear their religion on their chest are saying "Look how needy I am" so in sales one must use their religion to get their money. Example: pray with them whatever their religion to get the sale.

Simon Bar Legree: 1) a fictitious character made up by the writer of this book, 2) reprehensive, or representative of a real person unseen by the masses, 3) the darkest level of power any living human can obtain, 4) Satan that has tricked religious people to kill so he can control them.

Social Security Administration: the office that oversees the federal government's Ponzi scheme.

Speaking in tongues: 1) the art of speaking to God, 2) language of idiots, 3) created to fool the masses and take their money

Spin: lies created to mislead and deceive the public.

String Master: 1) title given to unseen corporate leaders (aka, puppeteers) who controls elected employees; 2) mafia, a thing per the FBI that does not exist

Stuffed suit: a well-dressed person with no personality, no fun to be with, drag to be around, knows it all and never smiles. His nick name could be *The Suit*.

Subsidies: welfare for the rich.

Superior Body: 1) a governing organization that Christian America must report to, 2) a corrupt group of world leaders bought by the top 85 people in the world, 3) the United Nations or UN

Super Hyper-Devaluation: 1) a thing that happens to all paper money or god/notes, 2) often called high inflation however there is no such thing as inflation, 3) end result of a poorly run country usually for God 4) a people or race stripped clean by the **BIG 3** that know what they are doing.

Tag: southern term for state license plate.

Take the car away: a sales gimmick to make the customer buy the car they want by taking it away and trying to sell them one they don't want.

Tashlich: is a ritual that many Jews observe during Rosh Ha Shanah. It means "casting off" in Hebrew and involves symbolically casting off the sins of the previous year by tossing pieces of bread or another food into a body of flowing water.

Taught Disorder – Brainwashed: religion

TDS Three Deadly Sins: dishonesty, felony, embarrassment.

(T/G): Remove time remove gravity

Theoretical physicist: 1.) Those who earn a living to not look at the universe before the big bang. 2.) Producer of nonsense and non-science. 3.) Title given by the pope to those who look at the universe after the big bang. Those who look before are in violation of blasphemy and will be stoned to death, impaled or burned at the stake for being a witch.

Time: Did not start with the big bang. It is found outside of universe, existed before the big bang.

Tire kicker: not real buyer, retired people killing time before early bird specials, lookers or lookyloos.

T.O.: *turn over*, action term, before a non-buying customer leaves the lot he/she must talk to a manager,

Too Highs: Vietnamese people or boat people never would buy a car, so you would avoid them, for inevitably they would say, "price to high,,, to high."

Trafficking in God: drug dealers of religion

White Gold: china from China

Ultimately: finally; in the end; At the most basic level.

Unicellular organism: Also known as single-cell.

Up: person, a buyer, a potential customer has come on the lot.

Upside down: a place one finds themselves after buying a car or truck on a big Taj Mahal lot.

W W P C S: abbreviation for Words White People Can't Say.

Wackos: people not like us.

Want-a-bees: non people, have no or bad credit.

Wants a car: distinction between needs and wants not as strong a buyer as *needs a car.*

Want-a-goes: term to describe an up that is trying to leave. "He has the want-a-goes."

White energy/white matter: "I"

White hole: Having mass but pushing out matter.

Whitey: a term given to white people that is to be offensive, but never is.

Young-gens: children raised by trash.

50/50 Warranty: a con pulled on the public that believe they are buying a car with half of the cost of repairs covered. Truth is, the car must be repaired at this store and repairs are inflated to 200% of true cost and the buyer pays 100% of the cost.

Socialosity

Books by William J Ryan

The Extermination of Kings, Part I
Journey to the Bay of Bengal - Revised

Two Tibetan monks witness the butchering and murder by the Chinese of all the inhabitants of a monastery in the Himalayas. As the only survivors and eyewitnesses, they face starvation as they are being hunted. They head south looking for sanctuary and are struck by the countless inhumanities they see and acts of destruction to the earth they love. *Available now*!

> ### *The Extermination of Kings, Part 1 – Screenplay*
> A version of the original book converted into a screenplay.

The Extermination of Kings, Part II
The Dark Continent

Word spreads of the only survivors and the monks receive help. Captain Jack, a big Irish seaman, gets them across the Indian Ocean and Osiris guides them across Africa through the perils they face there - man's inhumanity to man, foreign countries' trash and the consumption of all living things in order to survive. *Available Now!*

> ### *The Extermination of Kings, Part II – Screenplay* *Available!*

The Extermination of Kings, Part III
America

They are befriended by a billionaire that gets them to the land of the free but manipulates events for his own agenda. This is the last of the trilogy of easy to read fast-moving stories, with an outcome that helps the Tibetans gain power. *Available Now!*

The Extermination of Kings, Part III – Screenplay
Available!

Sheriff Jessy of Boonies, Kentucky 2007 Part I
An amusing and nostalgic look at an idyllic community and what happens when it is invaded by corrupt politicians. Sheriff Jessy tries to hold the community together in spite of black money and wins in the end. *Available now!*

Sheriff Jessy of Boonies, Kentucky Screenplay
Available!

Sheriff Jessy of Boonies, Kentucky 2009 Part II
Revenge of Dick and George, two boys from Texas
Politicians being what they are, bring an endless barrage of destruction to the community, with the goal of turning it into Lead Ville, USA. In their effort to destroy the community they expose Jessy and his dark secrets, with a tragic outcome. *Available soon!*

Levi's Reverse Wave Absorption
This is a riveting science fiction story about an Amish college student who invents a way to prevent earthquakes and pays for it with his life. As an FBI sting goes bad, corrupt Federal agents are exposed, taking you all the way to the top of the Government. *Available now!*

Screenplay - *Available!*

First Defense
Illegal drug trafficking across civilian lands, forces a community to defend themselves as the Federal Government looks the other way. *Warning: contains shocking solutions to real problems*, like Amy and her drill. *Available now!*

First Defense – Screenplay – *Available!*

The Good News Show
This is a scintillating scene by scene account of the news media, the control over the airwaves of American radio and television. With the unraveling of this empire comes a hard look at the future of our planet and the destruction that is coming. *Available now!*

The Good News Show - Screenplay *Available!*

Just Deserves
An in-depth look into life after death and the worlds beyond, from the vantage point of one who has just passed. Strange encounters and friendships develop as the earth reaches the end of its domination over man. *Available now!*
Just Deserves – Screenplay – *Available!*

The Copper Pit
A dramatic tale with an unlikely result of the President's and Congress's decision to banish outlawed street gangs to an abandoned copper mine in the middle of America's desert. *Available now!*
The Copper Pit – Screenplay – *Available!*

Seeds of Change
The story of a big city attorney who is forced by life events to move to a rural community which has been devastated by Federal Government programs like giving tax breaks to corporations that send American jobs overseas. A powerful political machine develops that changes the nation. *Available Now!*
Screenplay *Available!*

Letters to President Obama, 52 weeks 52 letters
Here is actual White House correspondence (with responses) and commentaries written by a common small-town businessman struggling in the 2010 depression. It reveals the author's transformation from a confused and frustrated citizen, to an awakened and empowered one. *Available now!*

Car Slugs
This is a disturbing look into the retail car sales industry through the eyes of one mentally over stimulated salesman. The story is set in the heyday of the 1990's, before the

destruction of our country by the banking industry. *Available Now!*

Car Slugs – Screenplay *Available!*

Scrupulosity *Revised*

Christianity is primarily used as examples of Scrupulosity levels One, Two, Three, and Four in this book, because of its power over this American government and its leaders, thereby all of us. The psychological disorder, Scrupulosity, is found by the author to be at a much more dangerous level than found in its classification, as a form of OCD (Obsessive compulsive disorder) for the author believes it manifests itself in the criminal behaviors of rape, murder, and genocide. There is a word describing these criminals of God and that word is Scrupulosity. *Available Now!*

Global Financial Super Heating

This is a dyslexic autodidacts' overview of most religions (afraid to live, afraid to die), resources, governments, their money, and the end of all life on earth if man continues to pretend that all is ok. The advantage of being an autodidact is that one is not encumbered with the knowledge of things taught, that one can or cannot do. It's all open for the author to share with you. With religions' blessings, the unregulated human population explosion is devastating this small planet and continues to leave only death and destruction as our legacies for future inhabitants. Lies from governments and religions and how 'The Big 3', controlled by the 85, are destroying the earth in pursuit of 'gods/notes' while the rest of us remain seemingly powerless. Right or wrong, are you prepared for what is to come? *Available now!*

In search for the "I"

My personal journey to understanding the complexities of all matter and the life it brings. From before the big bang to present day and back again. Life is a circle. How does the spirit of all life fit into all ordinary matter as we know it to be, beyond what we can see *The Complete Unified Circle Theory*. *Available Now!*

The Good Christian
A man finds a handwritten book amongst the belongings he found in a commercial storage shed he bought. This story takes you on two separate journeys of two different men that become intertwined by chance. One as a child that was raped by a priest suppresses the memories, and as an adult invokes vigilante justice. *Available now!*
The Good Christian – Screenplay – *Available!*

Amaton Man – Ask a tree for ages 6&Under Available!
Amaton Man – The Secret for ages 7 to 12 *Available!*
Amaton Man – The Price for ages 12 to 18 *Available!*
Amaton Man – A Brief History *Available!*
A series of coloring books meant to be used as a tool to aid in the fight against child sexual abuse. This coloring book is meant to help children, that have been or are being abused, to open up and tell someone, to empower them with the word, **"NO!"** in order to help them protect themselves. The stories within each of these books are meant for this purpose. *Available Now!*

The 3 Ks
A heart wrenching story based on a true double murder that happened in Tampa, Florida and the American Injustice System. Jon is a hardworking man trying to support his family and life a small portion of the American Dream. He comes home to find his wife and young daughter brutally murdered. After suffering the loss of his family, he is swept up in a life altering frame up that is perpetrated by blind and ruthless detectives in the Florida Justice System. The only thing that keeps him going is finding justice for his family and exposing the injustice that he had endured. *Available now!*
The 3 K's – Screenplay – *Available!*

Goyims
According to the Jewish religion, 98% of all people are not going to heaven and of the 2% that are going, they will go to heaven even if they don't believe in God. Regardless of your faith, regardless of your chosen god or gods, the outcome is the same; Armageddon. The faces of all man's Gods are but one and that is death in their names. *Available Now!*

Lords
A riveting drama about a historical religion fighting to reacquire its place in today's world, and love. The Lord King is a reincarnated God of the Aztecs, who fights to get back what once belonged to his people. Jan is a nurse who was once a tortured and abused child gets taken prisoner, but this prison is not at all what she expected. She finds peace from her past in an ancient ritual of freedom, and love. She is taken on a journey to a place she never believed she would see and finds herself as a Goddess. *Available Now!*
  ### Lords – Screenplay *Available now!*

Dr. Ghee
This is a gripping science fiction story about a family that struggles to live with Alzheimer's disease. You won't believe what lengths that they will go as they work towards the day that they will find a cure for this debilitating disease and save future generations. *Available now!*
  ### Dr. Ghee – Screenplay *Available now!*

Love and the Joy of Murder
A man and woman from seemingly opposite ends of society, find each other in the middle of a murder cover-up. This bazaar circumstance, narrated by the female victim, brings this unlikely pair together. They find that neither of them can or want to leave each other. From their closeness, love develops, as each of their personalities rub off on the other. They both

have finally found joy, love and happiness in each other on the fringes of life and the law. *Available Now!*

Love and the Joy of Murder – Screenplay

This screenplay was entered into the **Hollywood Screenwriting Competition in 2016** and was a finalist. **Placed 14th in the Action/Adventure feature category!**

Jesus Christ in Canaan

"Our race is the Master Race! We are divine gods on this planet. We are as different from the inferior races as they are from insects. In fact, compared to our race, other races are beasts and animals... cattle at best. Other races are considered as human excrement. Our destiny is to rule over the inferior races. Our earthly kingdom will be ruled by our leader with a rod of iron. The masses will lick our feet and serve us as our slaves"

These are just a few of the quotes that I have found that led me to investigate Jews and religion. I could not believe what I had found, so I wrote it down to pass it along to everyone. The stories within are true stories with some embellishment added to make them come alive to you, the reader. *Available Now!*

Dark Government

Beneath all governments are Dark Governments and their secretive networks to control and rule the world. This story is about what happens when the genetic growth of man is permitted to be altered and others move in to take control. *Available now!*

Dark Government - Screenplay Available!

Nature's Rights

If you are one of the many that believe everything is fine, this book is not for you. Most people think the experts know what they are doing and telling the public to fall in line like good little hand puppets. However the reality of the future of earth is not quite what we are being told. The questions I ask each one of you is, how will you survive? How will you feed your family? Where will you get water to drink? The big question is,,, when will this happen? This book is the author's attempt to show each reader willing to look into the future, the approximate time. It is very close. *Available!*

Grey Power – Project Term Limits

Have you ever thought about hurting someone that has hurt you, or thought about doing something to those in the government, because of the way that are running your country? If so, you need to read Grey Power ~ Project Term Limits.

When a world is on the brink of a catastrophic disaster and the people in power just don't want to take things seriously, what would you do?

Cooper has just retired from working at a bank and is very optimistic about his future. One day, everything changes and he becomes fed up with how those that are supposed to follow the rules persist on ignoring the rules that they don't like. He joins a very large group of people that have become fed up with how their country is being run, so they devise a plan to try to put things right. Cooper takes a trip that gives him a new lease on life in this harrowing tale of love, revenge, justice and peace at last. *Available now!*

Grey Power - Screenplay *Available!*

Aliens – What the hell is going on?

Life is not complicated, our defective split brains make this world full of riddles and we must rise above the confusion of our defective split brains.

Greedy people make things complicated to deliberately hide the truth. There is easy money to make for the few, if only a few know the truth. Knowledge is money and money is power and power can buy anything... like governments.

Today the rich flaunt their power over the rest of us in annual global meetings, showing off their religious symbols. Their power over us is unchallenged, because they own everything, including god and the future devastation as it's going on.

This book examines the hard facts of friendly aliens coming to earth over the past recent years. It is also of people behind governments that lie to their people to get the knowledge for new products of war that they can sell as their own invention.

Everything behind government is about power and money and the use of religion to control the masses. They will stop at nothing to keep control, power and money. It's just a big game to them. *Available now!*

Adina of Elysium

Adina of Elysium is an historical story about two green children found wandering outside of a town called Woolpit in England. I wrote this story using the historical information that I found through my investigation.

In a place called Elysium, where there are no wars, the sun is low in the sky and the land is green all the time. Adina and her brother Mawukura were out moving their herd, when a force from above spooks them. It forces them and the herd into a dark cave, where they waited in confusion, for what spooked them to leave.

When they finally emerge from the cave, they find themselves in a foreign land. It's so bright that they could barely see what lay before them and so hot that Adina thought she would burn. When her eyes adjust a bit, she sees a dead barren land and assumes it's the land of death.

Our green children have to try to adjust to this land of death, for they don't know if they will ever find their way home again. *Available now!*

Screenplay Available!

An Amber Intervention

One man's taught hatred of other religions and race's of people is abruptly altered in a flash of light. He is forever changed by this event and becomes a different person.

In his attempts to help change the Earth and warn its people of the Intervention that is to come, he meets many who try to obstruct his message. With the help of his sister and an old flame that has come back into his life, as well as a new friend called Amaton Man, who is from a planet far away, he has some small success.

With or without Jim's help, this intervention is to come regardless of what the Deceivers tell people. Jim's goals are to expose the criminal element that has taken over. The animal lust to have it all at any price is exposed, to help in part, bring out the kinder side of mankind that is so rarely seen. *Available!*

Screenplay – *Available!*

Oh God! Not Another Murder

This book is a parodies' of the endless murder mysteries coming from the BBC, regarding a small village in England. Where after a series of these stories, one is forced to think… "They must have killed off every inhabitant of this village. Who would want to live in a place where the murder rate is higher than living in gang infested Chicago or the city of L.A.?

Each week we are witness to yet another murder. The religious leader interferes with the bumbling inspector that never gets it right and constantly resents the unwanted help. But ultimately, this man standing next to God can find the true killers. Maybe its his divine magical powers that only this religion has and is supported by the government for controlling (brainwashing) the masses. *Available!*

Screenplay *Available!*

Deceivers – Invisible Masters and their Slaves

There is a secret organization that for hundreds of years have existed solely to obtain others land and riches by any means. War, murder, slavery, drug dealing and destruction of all other religions and their cultures are but a small part of the business models that they follow. To this day, these men hide behind governments and their corrupt politicians, moving freely, committing genocide for their chosen religion.

Most of these Deceivers embrace their god intensely for the sole purpose of enriching themselves. The few that truly believe in helping their fellow man are not advanced; they are removed or put to death. No one is to stand in their way.

Regardless of the pain, suffering and the extermination of those that stands in the way, their single goal is to control the slaves via religion and acquire wealth by any means possible. Rewriting history is easy when you own everything.

All those below the secret highest levels of this religious organization, inside as well as outside, are considered slaves. They are to do the bidding of the highest level people within this secretive cult. These "Lodges" around the world, enrich only the few while deceiving all others. This book exposes them; revealing their true agenda, money, wealth and power… using God.

Screenplay – *Available!*

The Gold Sphere

This is a story about a young girl finding a strange metallic orb after a wildfire. Follow this family as the find out what this orb can do and how it may help the planets future. *Available soon!*

Screenplay *Available!*

The Second Coming of Christ

The fallacy of the second coming of Christ is questioned only by the first. The thinking is… if it was true and the son of god did in fact come to Earth, things would be better.

God or the son of god would probably insist that the "Thou shall not kill" thing be enforced all over the planet for we are all (his children) the same, but it is not. Today man is killing man all over this planet for the sake of God. Can you imagine the shame he must carry when people are killing other people because of their belief in you? No wonder he does not show his face here. It would be filled with shame.

The total corruption of the galaxy called Kyklos, leaves the Nine Watchers no alternative but to end its existence. The 6th die off of all life is to come, but not at the hand of man, as predicted.

Only memories held by the living survivors of the Twin Experiment hold the truth of the hours of the last day of a planet called Earth, in a galaxy called Kyklos.   *Available soon!*

Change Change – The Perception of Vlaue

This book is being addressed to the current President of the United States, Donald J. Trump, the 45th president. It is the single goal and hope that somehow the spending and waste of tax dollars, enriching the few, will be exposed and ended.

We as individuals in the world have some power and that power is for us to lead government by example. Most all of us know that coins have no value; they are the pretense of value only. Business did this with the production of the Susan B. Anthony dollar that has led to billions of one dollar coins being produced but not being used by the people.

Change is only good for filling the holes in your driveway and filling up drawers and jars in our closets. Banks have all kinds of rules to take change back, they don't even want it, because it has no value and they make no money handling it.   *Available!*

God Religion and Pedophiles

Releasing the information within this book can get me killed. Within the pages of this book, I make every attempt to find the truth among all of the lies that we have been told all of our lives. These words on paper are not about hate mongering of one or any religion or that of any god, but to find the truth that eludes most all people. Most all governments use religions and have done horrific things since we, as a race, came out of the dark ages and into the light of modern present times. Few among these particular religions will admit their participation (blind faith) in genocide. At best, they somehow will justify their religions actions (as if it were possible). All of us who live on this planet have been lied to all of our lives (by the Deceivers), in order to trick and deceive us and then take advantage of our ignorance. One of these Deceivers said..."If they knew the truth, they would kill us."Religion is always used as leverage to create anger and hate by de-humanizing people, making it easier to kill them. Religion is the true enemy of "We the People"... not God.

Available Now!

Available now through Amazon.com and other fine retail book stores